Collaboration Tools for Project Managers

How to Choose, Get Started, and Collaborate with Technology

By Elizabeth Harrin

Library of Congress Cataloging-in-Publication Data

Names: Harrin, Elizabeth, author.
Title: Collaboration tools for project managers : how to choose, get started,
   and collaborate with technology / by Elizabeth Harrin.
Description: Newton Square, PA : Project Management Institute, Inc., 2016.
Identifiers: LCCN 2016011142 | ISBN 9781628251135 (pbk. : alk. paper)
Subjects: LCSH: Project management. | Social media. | Information
   technology—Management
Classification: LCC HD69.P75 .H3588 2016 | DDC 658.4/04—dc23
LC record available at https://lccn.loc.gov/2016011142

ISBN: 978-1-62825-113-5

Published by: Project Management Institute, Inc.
            14 Campus Boulevard
            Newtown Square, Pennsylvania 19073-3299 USA
            Phone: +6100-356-4600
            Fax: +610-356-4647
            Email: customercare@pmi.org
            Internet: www.PMI.org

PMI Publications welcomes corrections and comments on its books. Please feel free to send comments on typographical, formatting, or other errors. Simply make a copy of the relevant page of the book, mark the error, and send it to: Book Editor, PMI Publications, 14 Campus Boulevard, Newtown Square, PA 19073-3299 USA.

To inquire about discounts for resale or educational purposes, please contact the PMI Book Service Center.

            PMI Book Service Center
            P.O. Box 932683, Atlanta, GA 31193-2683 USA
            Phone: 1-866-276-4764 (within the U.S. or Canada) or
            +1-770-280-4129 (globally)
            Fax: +1-770-280-4113
            Email: info@bookorders.pmi.org

10 9 8 7 6 5 4 3 2 1

Table of Contents

Acknowledgments xiii

Foreword xv

Introduction 1
    The Reason for This Book 2
    Considering Collaboration Tools:
       Project Management Software Evolved 3
    How the Book is Organized.. 4
    Is This Book for You?.. 5

Part 1: The Context for Collaboration...7

Chapter 1: Why We Are Leaving Behind
Old Working Practices...9
    1. Project timescales require frequent collaboration.................................11
    2. Virtual teams need better tools. 11
    3. Being digital and social drives business results.................................12
    4. It's the way business works today. 13
    Beyond Project Teams 15
    Summary..15

Chapter 2: Online Collaboration: The New Normal 17
    Communicating Online: A Brief History.. 17
    Moving Your Team Online...18
       1. Community 19
       2. Communication 19
       3. Access to data 20
       4. Connectivity 21

Technology for Collaboration.. 23

   Virtual Factor 1: Geography... 24

   Virtual Factor 2: Electronic Communication........................... 25

   Virtual Factor 3: Culture.. 25

The Limitations of Online Collaboration.. 26

Summary... 26

Chapter 3: Collaboration Tools 101 27

   1. Instant Messaging.. 28

      Why should I use this feature?.. 29

      Pros 29

      Cons 31

   2. File upload 31

      Why should I use this feature?.. 31

      Pros 32

      Cons 32

   3. File versioning and collaboration 34

      Why should I use this feature?.. 34

      Pros 34

      Cons 35

   4. Create groups/teams...35

      Why should I use this feature?..35

      Pros 35

      Cons 36

   5. Share updates 36

      Why should I use this feature?.. 36

      Pros 37

      Cons 37

   6. Search...37

      Why should I use this feature?..37

      Pros 38

      Cons 38

7. Reports 38

   Why should I use this feature? 38

   Pros 39

   Cons 39

8. Workflows 39

   Why should I use this feature? 40

   Pros 40

   Cons 40

9. Notifications and alerts 40

   Why should I use this feature? 41

   Pros 41

   Cons 41

10. Liking and gamification 41

   Why should I use this feature? 42

   Pros 42

   Cons 42

The Disadvantages of Collaboration Tools 43

Summary 44

**Chapter 4: Communication and the
Project Management Life Cycle** 45

The Project Management Life Cycle: The Communication View 45

   Initiation Phase 46

   Planning Phase 47

   Delivery Phase(s) 48

   Closure Phase 49

Communication Challenges for Project Managers
(And How You Can Address Them) 51

   1. Communicating up and out to stakeholders and sponsors 51

   2. Managing miscommunication 52

   3. Communicating for team building 53

   4. Managing the team's communication preferences 54

Summary 56

Chapter 5: Team Management and the Project Management Life Cycle 57

The Project Management Life Cycle: The Team Management View........ 57

Initiation Phase...60

Planning Phase...61

Delivery Phase(s) 63

Closure Phase 66

Team Management Challenges 66

1. Managing dispersed teams...67

2. Managing across cultures 68

3. Managing part-time team members 70

4. Managing people who don't work for you 71

Summary..73

Part 2: Making It Work...75

Chapter 6: Strategy First 77

Strategy Before Tools...78

Developing a Strategy 79

Step 1: Identify the problems..79

Step 2: Identify stakeholders..79

Step 3: Define your goals..80

Step 4: Identify possible solutions. 81

Defining What You Want from Your Software 81

1. Functional Requirements..83

2. Nonfunctional Requirements 86

3. Vendor Fit 88

4. Cost...90

5. Other Strategic Elements 90

The Question of Gamification...90

Summary..92

Chapter 7: Is Your Team Ready to Work Online?.......................... 93

Four Dependencies for a Successful Deployment............................ 93

Team Culture: Is Your Team Ready?.. 94

Using Social Technographics for Profiling 96

Project Culture: How are You Going to Pilot Your Software? 99

The Timescales...99

The Criticality 100

The Objectives.. 100

Organization Culture: What Else is Your Company Doing? 101

Appetite 101

Current Activity.. 101

Personal Culture: How Much Time Do You Have to
Dedicate to Making this Work? 102

Managing the Time Required 102

Your Level of Commitment 103

Communicate, Communicate, Communicate 105

Summary..106

Chapter 8: Winning Over Management **107**

Prepare the Ground...108

Identifying Risks 109

Measure Success 110

Dispel Myths..111

Myth #1: It's a Big Change 111

Myth #2: Anyone Can Do Anything...112

Myth #3: Wikis are Problematic..112

Myth #4: No More Face-To-Face Meetings....................................112

Myth #5: It Will Waste Time 113

Myth #6: We Can Monitor Individual Activity..................................114

Dealing with Lack of Support..115

Summary..116

Chapter 9: How to Choose and Use the Right Tools **117**

First. . .Decide..117

Developing a Business Case...118

The Alternative to a Financial Business Case 119

First Steps for Implementation 120

Planning Your Pilot 120

Treat It Like a Project..121

Plan and Schedule..121

Review Configuration Options 122

Going Live.. 124

Making it Easy to Use... 126

Evaluating the Benefits 128

What Happens If Take-Up is Poor?.. 129

Is There a Culture of Sharing? 129

Stakeholder Mapping: What are They Missing? 131

Easier Access to the Tool... 131

Are There Other Issues in the Team?...................................... 131

Set a Good Example 132

Make it Fun... 132

Make it Useful 132

Buddy Up.. 132

Blend Old and New.. 133

Summary.. 134

**Chapter 10: Getting Started With
Collaboration Tools: Using Wikis... 135**

Wikis Explained 135

The Advantages of Wikis... 136

Wiki Disadvantages 137

Wikis as Organizational Knowledge Repositories 138

Wikis for Lessons Learned 139

First Steps With Wikis 140

Choose and Install Your Tools... 141

Look and Feel 142

Empower Your Authors... 142

Review Regularly 142

Dealing With Revisions 144

Subscribe.. 144

Search... 144

Wiki Mistakes.. 145

Anonymity: The Big No-No... 145

Perfection: Don't Bother... 146

Topics: Step Back When Necessary 146

Irrelevance: Letting the Wiki Go Stale 146

Wiki Best Practices...146

Summary...147

Chapter 11: Managing Online Culture Shock:
Risk Mitigation Strategies for Collaborating Online......................149

Managing the Overload 149

Filtering 150

Segment the Conversations...151

Promoting Value 151

Managing the "Experts" 152

Relevancy..152

Giving a Voice to the Many...153

Managing the "Always On" Culture...154

Mobile Solutions 155

Managing the Lack of Control 155

Managing Expectations 156

Online Etiquette...157

Summary...158

Chapter 12: Keeping Your Project Data Secure.................................161

Start at the Beginning: Usage Policies 161

Policies on Archiving 163

Educate Your Team...164

Legal Issues..164

Addressing Security Concerns..165

1. Access Control 165

2. Back Ups...167

3. Audit Trails 167

4. Abuses of the System...168

5. Unauthorized Software..169

Summary...169

Part 3: The Bigger Picture 171

Chapter 13: Building Personal Online Credibility 173
   Getting Started 173
   Creating an Online Profile..175
      Photos..177
      Nothing is Private! 177
      The Risk of Digital Sharecropping...178
   Social Media for Continuing Professional Development 179
   The Power of Twitter 180
   Social Recruiting: The Job Search Moves Online 181
      Help With Interview Preparation 182
   Being Credible 184
      The Company You Keep...185
   Pay Attention to the Little Things 186
   Summary..186

Chapter 14: Conclusions: The Future of Work 189
   Looking Forward: Seven Future Trends..194
      1. Project Analytics 194
      2. Digital PMOs and the Role of the Digital Leader 195
      3. The Culture of Collaboration 195
      4. Interoperability 196
      5. Interoperability of Methodology 197
      6. Archiving 197
      7. Predictive Software 198
   Summary..198

Appendix: Project Management Resources Online..........................201

Glossary 205

References..209

Suggested Reading 215

About the Author 217

Praise for Collaboration Tools for Project Managers 219

Acknowledgments

A book about collaboration involves a lot of collaboration, and I have been very grateful to have input from many individuals. I'd like to specifically mention Simon Hird, Brett Harned, Liz Pearce and Tatyana Sussex, Lindsay Scott, Dave Shirley, Dave Garrett, Dave Bryde, and Christina Unterhitzenberger. Many companies generously gave up their time to talk to me about their use of social media and collaboration tools for getting work done, some of which did not make it into the book, but were incredibly valuable conversations.

I'm also grateful to the publishing division of the Project Management Institute, especially Barbara Walsh for her support throughout this process and Kim Shinners for her expert attention to detail. The book has been extensively proofread and reviewed, so any errors or omissions in it are strictly my own.

Finally, I'd like to thank my family for their support along the way: My parents, Pauline and Alan, especially Mum for her help with proofreading and editing again.

And for Jon, Jack, and Oliver. Of course.

Foreword

Today, tools like Slack, Google Hangouts, and Basecamp are exploding in popularity. These applications facilitate fluid interaction for teams who work remotely from far-flung locations, who telecommute, and even teammates sharing the same physical work space.

According to a Microsoft survey,[1] 46% of workers say that their productivity has greatly or somewhat increased because of social media use in the office, and more than one-third (37%) say that they could do their job *better* if their organization's management was more on-board in the use of social tools in the workplace. So, it is clear that the use of social media is not just a trend to watch; it is rapidly becoming a major success factor for business.

The broader trends are also compelling. People are generally spending twice as much time online as they did a decade ago[2] and more than a quarter of that time is dedicated to social networking.[3] As project teams skew younger and grow more distributed, as telecommuting options increase, project teams are likely to spend more time online than face to face. The trick is for project leaders to use technology to bring people together in ways that not only replicate face-to-face collaboration, but also enhance it.

This book will help project managers lay a solid foundation for virtual collaboration that:

- Saves time, by simplifying interactions
- Reduces risk and stress through well-timed, deeper, more focused discussions with targeted audiences
- Speeds decision making in ways that lead to project success

---

[1] Bennett, S. (2013, June 26). Social media increases productivity, but management still resistant, says study. *Adweek*. Retrieved 8 February 2016 from http://www.adweek.com/socialtimes/social-media-workplace-survey/486874?red=at
[2] OfCom for Consumers. (n. d.). Retrieved 8 February 2016 from http://consumers.ofcom.org.uk/news/time-spent-online-doubles/
[3] Bennett, S. (2015, January 27). 28% of time spent online is social networking. *Adweek*. Retrieved 8 February 2016 from http://www.adweek.com/socialtimes/time-spent-online/613474

Author Elizabeth Harrin is an active project leader with direct experience using these tools for project management and a subject matter expert that thousands turn to for guidance. On ProjectManagement.com and at events like the PMI® Global Congress, she is well known for her sage advice and quick answers to a broad range of questions about social media, new technology, and virtual collaboration. After reading the book, be sure to connect with Elizabeth online. In total, this book combined with Elizabeth's personalized advice will help you to lead a major change in your organization.

The fact that you have picked up this book means you feel a need to use virtual collaboration tools more effectively. You likely feel the pain of being behind the collaboration curve and aren't sure where to start. But now is the time and this book is the starting point. Using these tools and approaches will yield immediate, tangible results for your project team and your organization.

Dave Garrett, Director of Digital Presence,
Project Management Institute

Introduction

When an earlier version of this book was released under the title, *Social Media for Project Managers*, it focused on how mainstream social media tools could be used in the workplace to engage teams and create collaboration and participation on projects. Just a few years on, the working environment has changed significantly.

I've reflected that in this current book, *Social Media for Project Managers* has been fully revised and updated and in that process, it morphed into something quite different. While there are hundreds of little changes, new examples, and updated research, the two crucial differences are:

First, the language has changed. For example, we are no longer talking about creating our own project wikis, but rather using collaboration tools designed for the purpose of working with virtual teams that have wiki functionality inherent in the tool. Today, the discussion is about how project management has adopted social media-style technology and incorporated it into the tools used to get work done. This has happened because project management software has caught up with what teams actually need to manage in complex, virtual environments.

Another byproduct of the software now in use for adopting the functionality of social networks is that the debate has shifted from "should we adopt new communication methods" to "how should we adopt new communication methods." Rather than a discourse on the benefits, project managers need practical guides about how to choose and use collaboration tools.

Second, project managers have changed. The role of the project manager is expanding to include managing change and getting involved earlier and earlier in the project process. With that in mind, there is a need to discuss how to select a tool and prepare the business case for introducing collaboration software. I've dedicated a large chunk of the book to establishing a team collaboration software strategy and providing information on how to execute that strategy through creating a robust business case and implementing your software.

The Reason for This Book

Over the last few years, a not-very-subtle change has happened in the workplace. Project managers no longer manage tasks and people; they create collaborative environments where people can do their very best work to achieve corporate goals.

It's not management-speak. It's the difference between task management and engaging team members. It's the difference between command-and-control and working together as equals. It's also not a new idea, but one made more acute by multigenerational teams.

In parallel, digital culture has exploded, fundamentally changing the operating model of many businesses and the way consumers engage with products and services. This has recently spilled over into how projects are managed, but this isn't really a new idea either.

Fifteen years ago, Richard Murch, in his book, *Project Management: Best Practices for IT Professionals*, predicted that we would be using the Internet to support project communications as well as recruitment and training of project managers. He called it I-PM: Internet Project Management (Murch, 2001). Among other things, he believed that the Internet would enable project managers to automate the capture of project information and enable electronic collaboration.

Let's just say that it's taken project management a while to catch up, but now the change is happening and it's happening fast. Research from MIT Sloan reports that the number one reason cited by CIOs for using social business tools like online collaboration software is for managing projects (Kiron, Palmer, Nguyen Phillips, & Berkman, 2013).

Collaboration at work, as most people would understand it, is what we do every day now. Projects are collaborative by nature, with people from various departments and companies forming a temporary organizational structure and working together to achieve a common objective.

The collaborative workplace is about more than this day-to-day kind of working together. Instead, it fosters sharing our collective knowledge, skills, and resources and integrating disparate contributions into a productive whole. Don Tapscott and Anthony D. Williams call the potential to deliver greatness through this way of working "the new promise of collaboration" in their book, *Wikinomics: How Mass Collaboration Changes Everything* (Tapscott & Williams, 2008). They believe, as do others, that opening up the knowledge channels and promoting cross-organizational sharing will be the way in which organizations will generate wealth in the future. Project leaders need to be at the forefront of this organizational change to support our companies with innovative projects going forward.

However, collaboration is hard. You work with teams across many locations, organizations, and cultures. You manage many projects at once and work with colleagues who have no formal background in project management or any desire to use the "professional" enterprise project management tools that many Baby Boomer project managers trained in.

If you want to help your teams collaborate more effectively, save yourself some time, and reduce your stress levels, then this book is for you.

It aims to demystify the use of collaboration tools for project teams. It will help you choose and deploy a software solution that is right for you, taking into account the needs of your team, your business case, and the security and management challenges that you will need to address.

If you already have collaboration tools in use, it will help you scale them up across your project management office or enterprise, and get more out of them through driving better adoption and best practices.

Considering Collaboration Tools: Project Management Software Evolved

Project software used to be the domain of the project manager. Tasks and milestones were stored and reported, but project management software provided little, if any, insight into the "doing" of the tasks and the decisions taken along the way. Collaboration tools make this visible to everyone by improving transparency across the whole team. You don't have to be a software whiz to use them.

However, project management itself hasn't fundamentally changed. Project managers have always been primarily focused on creating participation in projects. Knowing how to engage people has always been part of that—if somewhat overlooked in the literature and standards until recently. Collaboration technologies are another way to do that.

I first got interested in this as a topic when I started working in healthcare. The speed of advancements in healthcare technology is incredible and the pace of change in the healthcare arena made me realize how slow the pace of change is in project management. I've been pleasantly surprised to see the shift in working practices so acutely, although I expect many businesses are slower to adopt new methods.

Collaboration tools are a new method that may not feel comfortable or appropriate right now. But other people, our project stakeholders and team members, are using them, and that makes it a good idea to find out what they are all about. After all, even if you feel they are a waste of time, you won't personally reverse the technology trend just by ignoring it. As with all project management tools and methods, you have to know the rules before you can start ignoring them.

How the Book is Organized

This book has three parts. In the first part, we look at the context for collaboration, how technology can support collaborative working, and how it fits into the project management life cycle.

The second part covers how you can make technology for collaboration work in practice through defining your strategy and engaging the team in the change. It also covers practical suggestions for security and managing the "culture shock" of shifting to new ways of working.

Part 3 discusses the bigger picture of collaboration technology and social media at work. We cover personal credibility and safety online as well as job hunting and online professional development. The final chapter offers a nonexhaustive view of what the future of collaboration and technology might have to offer project leaders by considering current trends.

One of the issues in writing about technology is that it moves on quickly. It is quite probable that some of the software and tools described here have been overtaken by newer, better tools by the time you read this. In fact, some of the companies may no longer exist: The web is a rapidly changing environment. No matter. Use the product names as placeholders: They are signposts pointing toward a concept, and it is the concept that is important, not the corporate embodiment of it. Change and innovation in the social media and collaboration space are good things. Change normally means that tools are improving, becoming more robust and useful.

Whatever technology product you use to drive collaboration, the examples of how other companies are doing it will still be of use to you. Throughout the book, you will find examples of companies and individuals using social media tools to improve their project practices. Where I haven't included a reference for the source of an anecdote, it has come from a personal interview specifically for this book.

Is This Book for You?

This book is aimed at project, program, and portfolio managers, whether you work for a large or small company or in the public or private sector. If you are interested in finding out more about how you can use technology like wikis, instant messaging, and collaboration tools on your projects, then this book is for you. It will also be of use if your company has already chosen a suite of enterprise tools, as it will give you the skills and vocabulary you need to be able to tap into that effectively.

In this book, you'll discover the reasons why project leaders should get on board with online collaboration and technology for virtual working. It also offers practical guidance on the use of such tools for working effectively with others on projects.

I look forward to joining you on your tour through the tools of online work and hope that you take away the knowledge you need to transform your organization, one project at a time.

The Context for Collaboration

Part 1 looks at the sea change in working practices. It examines the ways in which the project management landscape has evolved to operate online and provides a contextual background for how collaboration tools can be used for getting work done.

It includes the following chapters:

- Chapter 1: Why We Are Leaving Behind Old Working Practices
- Chapter 2: Online Collaboration: The New Normal
- Chapter 3: Collaboration Tools 101
- Chapter 4: Communication and the Project Management Life Cycle
- Chapter 5: Team Management and the Project Management Life Cycle

Why We Are Leaving Behind Old Working Practices

When *Social Media for Project Managers* was first published in 2010, the idea of using online tools and web technology for enhancing productivity on project teams was relatively new. Today, it feels as if everyone's doing it.

Much more of our working and personal lives is run online and, for the youngest generations in the workforce, it's the only working practice they have ever known. Part of the shift away from the old options for collaboration has to do with the fact that there are fewer people around who want to work that way anymore. Why use a conference bridge when a group Skype call gives you more data about your recipients and allows for chat and document sharing with the group while you're speaking?

The old ways of working aren't even that old. You don't have to be nearing retirement to remember fax machines and internal forums. Everyone has a story about a "command and control" style manager and we can all have a laugh at how dated that approach to management seems today.

Gartner's commentary on digital business concludes that this shift has come about due to what they call the Nexus of Forces (Howard et al., 2014). Four technology trends make up the Nexus. These are Social, Mobile, Cloud, and Information. Let's dig into that jargon now:

1. **Social**
   This reflects the move toward servant-leadership and collaborative, matrixed, and flat teams as a way to achieve corporate objectives. The move away from the brochure-ware, static pages of the Internet toward a more interactive and

personalized feel to browsing is one of the symptoms of this trend.

2. **Mobile**
   Mobile technology offers much more than just the ability to make calls and access data on the go. For project managers, who are often highly mobile workers, this takes data access to a level beyond just updating a project plan from the airport. The development of location-based data services and social tools that offer contextual information (e.g., "Find my nearest. . .") frames the data in a way that is personally relevant and useful at that moment.

3. **Cloud**
   Cloud solutions offer businesses scalable, rapid-deployment applications without high infrastructure costs. Routine backups, frequent updates, and high uptime are other advantages. The cloud works with both desktop and mobile environments, making it a highly efficient and flexible way to work. Or, as a manager of mine once said, "Someone else's computers plus tax."[1]

4. **Information**
   You may have heard of "big data." It describes the vast amounts of data that companies collect about their customers and transactions and how this can be processed into business intelligence. Effective analysis and use of this information, whether it relates to the turnaround time for dealing with project risks or what you buy in the supermarket, becomes a way of differentiating businesses from the competition.

Gartner concludes that these four trends allow businesses to

- improve how they interact with customers;
- launch new products;
- create points of difference from competitors;
- reach new customer markets; and
- improve efficiency across the operations.

---

[1] My thanks to Phil Peplow for this insight.

However, just because the technology is there, doesn't mean project teams have to use it, and traditional project management has been slower than other areas of business to adopt new working practices and methods.

Today, project teams are making the shift and it hasn't been subtle. Supported by technology, change is being driven by business and social imperatives. We're leaving behind the old ways of working for four reasons:

1. Project timescales drive the need for frequent collaboration.
2. Digital tools are better options for virtual teams.
3. Digital tools have been shown to help businesses get better results.
4. Society moves on: We don't have stone wheels on our carts any longer and now, the trend for collaboration is to do it online.

Let's look at those in more detail.

1. Project timescales require frequent collaboration.

Project team meetings have gone from weekly affairs to daily stand ups to twice-daily check-ins. The speed that business takes place at, and the pace of change, means that the old ways that project teams used to get together and report progress just aren't effective any longer. Teams need faster, re-al-time (or near real-time) access to information and each other.

There is now an inherent understanding in many businesses that in order to meet the needs of modern project management, business practices have to change. It's not rocket science that collaboration tools should help teams collaborate: That's what they are supposed to do. They tend to be a cost-effective solution for many companies looking for alternatives to lead and manage project teams. The take-up in many areas is already there, recognizing this need: The major use of social tools at work, according to CIOs in a study published by Deloitte University Press, is to manage projects (Kiron et al., 2013).

2. Virtual teams need better tools.

Today's business teams don't work in a face-to-face environment all the time. That's simply not a practical way to get work done when you want to access the best and most cost-effective talent from across the world. Project managers have to tap into other solutions in order to deal with virtuality. There's more about what it means to work virtually in Chapter 2.

A 2014 survey of over 1,200 European project managers by software company Projectplace reports that 37% of respondents say that lack of communication between team members is their main collaboration challenge (Projectplace, n.d.). Nearly a third of project managers say that it's hard to know which communication channel they should be using on a daily basis.

Virtual teams have it even harder: 22% of respondents in that study report that they can't find the time to "meet" on a conference call or in-person. Inefficiencies in collaboration and project management costs teams between two and three hours a week, equating to 20 days lost per year.

Microsoft Office and email are no longer suitable for managing projects, although some would argue that they never were. Collaboration tools move project teams along the efficiency scale and deliver benefits to virtual and colocated teams. According to the Projectplace research:

- 82% of project managers report that better project management tools result in more time saved
- 80% say that tools reduce their stress levels
- 71% report a stronger sense of team morale
- 69% report better control of project costs

It's important to balance these figures with the disruptive influence of technology as well. The study also shows that two thirds of project managers can access sensitive data; data that they probably shouldn't have access to. Yet only a little over half of them have a software solution that manages version control for documentation, which has the potential to cause issues and confusion. Security and data management are covered in more detail in Chapter 12.

3. Being digital and social drives business results.

Digital tools have been shown to drive better business results. According to a study by McKinsey (Bughin & Chui, 2010), the main business benefits for companies using collaboration tools are:

- increased speed of access to knowledge (77% of respondents reported this);
- reduced cost of communication (60%);

- increased speed of access to internal subject matter experts (52%); and
- reduced travel costs (44%).

This report also shows that companies using collaboration and digital tools internally are:

- more likely to lead their market sector;
- reporting greater market share than their competitors; and
- using management practices that result in higher margins.

Another study concludes that collaboration tools have the potential to raise the productivity of a knowledge worker by 20% to 25% (Chiu et al., 2012). And yet another study, this time by Cap Gemini, concludes that companies that truly understand how to drive value through digital transformation are 26% more profitable than their industry competitors (Westerman, Tannou, Bonnet, Ferraris, & McAfee, n.d.).

In a project environment, the results are similar. In *Managing the Urgent and Unexpected*, a book of 12 case studies about projects that were kicked off in emergency situations, Stephen Wearne and Keith White-Hunt write about the lessons learned from those projects. They frequently refer to the fact that collaborative working and cooperative attitudes drove project success, often in extremely difficult situations (Wearne & White-Hunt, 2014).

Even if you like to take a relatively cynical view of research like this, the data is pretty compelling. When you think about it, tools that make it easier to work together are, logically, likely to take costs out of businesses and speed up delivery.

4. It's the way business works today.

In the past—and it wasn't that long ago—the monthly steering group report would be an adequate representation of the project status. It was acknowledged that it was not a real-time project position, but it was accurate enough for the purposes of judging progress against milestones and budget. This data would be sufficient for the steering group, and if anyone else wanted a formal project status report, the latest steering group report could be handed over as a snapshot in time. Most of the time, people were happy with this level of detail, even though, implicitly, they knew it could no longer be true. Only in an emergency would anyone ask to see anything more up-to-date.

Today, project stakeholders have different expectations about project information, because they can get *other* information at the click of button. You want to know the weather in Bangalore? Google it. You want real-time stock prices on the Nikkei? Google it. You want up-to-date project status reports? Here's last month's steering group report, precisely 19 days out-of-date. This lack of real-time data is no longer acceptable to project stakeholders who can get everything else in a fraction of a second.

Project stakeholders expect real-time, up-to-date status reports. As a minimum, they expect you to give them that information whenever they ask for it, by return of email. Project managers now have to deal with those raised expectations and always be on top of project status in case anyone asks. Of course, they always should have been on top of the project status. The difference now is that it has to be transparent instead of in your head.

Google has shaped our expectations around the availability of real-time data. The availability of hardware has also been a factor in changing how stakeholders interact with each other and the project data. Cell phones and tablets now let you carry your office in your pocket. A complex, color-coded project spreadsheet might look great from a laptop screen, but becomes incredibly difficult to decipher on a 2×2 inch screen. Hyperconnectivity—the way in which individuals, machines, and data are linked by the Internet—has fundamentally changed our society and by default, the way in which project teams work.

Generation Y (also known as Millennials) make up those in your workplace born after 1987 and are among the most mobile, flexible, and connected. They have grown up with the web and the interactivity it provides. They manage their social lives on Facebook and they join dynamic online communities. This group is bringing their natural ways of interacting with others through technology into the workplace and, in many cases, they are finding that their employers are not able to keep up with their requirements for speed and innovation.

We're seeing the social trends of online collaboration spill over into the workplace. Research by Callum Dolan points out that in IT and change projects, businesses are seeing high use of collaborative project tools, but the collaboration trend is touching other industries too. Scientific research projects, for example, favor content communities over other tools, reflecting the requirement for publication and searching of data sets (Dolan, 2013).

A practical benefit of this trend is that collaboration tools can serve as a knowledge repository. The Project Management Institute's *Project Management Talent Gap* report (PMI, 2013) concludes that over 15 million new project management roles will be created over a ten-year period. The retiring Baby Boomer generation will also be stepping down from senior project roles during this time. The knowledge transfer between the experienced project managers leaving the workplace and the influx of new, inexperienced project managers could be helped by building up organizational knowledge about projects now.

Beyond Project Teams

The project management role is all about communication and working with other people to get things done. In many cases, project managers don't have direct line management responsibility for the teams they lead, so they juggle complex relationships and organizational politics. It is really important that project managers are perceived to be people with whom it is easy to work: Nobody wants to get stuck on a project headed up by someone who is known in the company as difficult.

Project teams are often drawn from multiple departments, providing a cross-functional base made up of different skills and backgrounds. On a project, managing the range of different personalities can be enough of a challenge. However, now project managers are facing new challenges: People drawn from different teams have different experiences of the work environment and what that means to them. In other words, some of the teams you work with will have adopted collaboration tools a while ago. Virtual working will be commonplace for some of your colleagues and unheard of for others. Project managers need to be able to converge the working styles and preferences for multiple individuals into a cohesive project team environment.

Collaboration tools can provide a common platform among teams, departments, and organizations that create a level playing field and make it easy to work together.

Summary

Project managers rely on communication and team management skills all the time. The fast pace of change, which is created by converging technical trends and business drivers that move organizations toward

CHAPTER 2

Online Collaboration: The New Normal

In Chapter 1, we saw that the world of work is changing and that online collaboration is the way that the most productive companies get work done. You're interested in finding out how these technologies can help you manage your projects more effectively. That's why you have picked up this book.

We'll cover a lot of ground in the subsequent chapters about how you can choose and implement digital tools in your workplace to support your project management practices. But first, let's look at what we are actually talking about when we refer to collaboration. What do we hope our teams will do better or differently if they have technology to help them on their projects?

Communicating Online: A Brief History

Social media, social networking, and online collaboration may sound like new terms, but people have been using the Internet to communicate with each other since the 1980s. Admittedly, the early bulletin board systems and chat rooms were not terribly sophisticated, but they did allow people to leave each other messages. That's communication. As the technology for building websites became easier to use, the Internet evolved from a place where techie experts shared bits of code to a domain where anyone could publish anything.

Humans are predisposed to connect with each other, and as the barriers to entry were reduced, participation grew. We like communities and we like being a part of something; we're social animals. Along with the dot-com boom of the 1990s, came technology to help us do that and to make it easier to smarten up the hideous websites we had been building previously. Blogger and LiveJournal—two hugely successful blogging platforms—were launched in 1999, and by 2003, blogging was a recognized pastime, with many businesses hosting their own corporate blogs for marketing purposes.

At the same time, faster Internet connections became available and businesses and home-users started switching to connections that didn't take five minutes to download one page. Suddenly, easy to use technology and widespread take-up of broadband meant that millions of people were online, ready to talk and collaborate with each other.

Whether it is an old-style forum, a tiny personal blog, or a structured corporate collaboration tool: They are all opportunities for us to connect with other people.

However, the speedy rise in online communication hasn't worked seamlessly. "As a general rule," writes Phil Simon in his book, *Message Not Received* (Simon, 2015), "the quality and clarity of business communication have deteriorated considerably over the past 10 years." Project teams will recognize that jargon, an over-reliance on email, and working under considerable time pressure have all contributed to miscommunications at one time or another.

There has been considerable benefit gained from online communications and, with caution, there is more yet to come.

Moving Your Team Online

Project managers can tap into the human need to want to connect and participate by using social and collaborative tools to bring project teams together virtually.

A simple definition of collaboration is "to work with others to get something done." When you collaborate, you:

- Communicate with another person, team, or group, potentially including third parties or other organizations
- Share a common purpose
- Achieve something

Collaboration could be seen as a fancy new label for "teamwork," but I think it goes further than that. Teamwork doesn't include the option of working with people outside your team. Today, many project teams rely on external parties, such as suppliers, who also play their part. Teamwork doesn't adequately reflect the level of creativity, knowledge sharing, and debate that collaboration offers. Teamwork implies working under the direction of a team leader, whereas collaboration often takes place in nonhierarchical situations.

There are four things that underpin digital collaboration in a project team environment:

1. Community: A sense of community and trust in that community
2. Communication: Effective and timely
3. Access to data: Relevant data for making decisions and reporting
4. Connectivity: Ability to access data and expertise from any-where, at any time

Without these, project managers will find it hard to get the team working together to deliver the shared vision. Let's look at each of those in turn.

1. Community

When groups of people come together with a common objective, you end up with a sense of community almost by default. However, what creates a true and trusting community is the ability to interact with each other. This is something that the web allows us to do more so than any other form of media. You can ring in to a radio show, or write a letter to the editor of your daily newspaper, but traditional forms of media don't engender community.

You can find communities for all kinds of things online, from PMI's virtual communities on various facets of project management to independent groups talking about green project management, critical chain project management, or anything else. Online tools allow groups of like-minded people to come together, and project managers can tap into this. After all, your project team is like-minded, with a common objective—to deliver your project.

2. Communication

Online tools are hugely beneficial to the way in which we communicate information because they provide more options for project teams to use.

Collaboration tools also offer a greater ability to personalize and tailor messages through bespoke home pages, data feeds, group membership, and dashboards.

Instead of one message to everyone, you can slice your audience into groups and provide them with targeted communication, which is more likely to be interpreted and understood the way you intended.

Communication also needs to be honest and transparent, and this is something that should underpin all your project messages, whether via your digital tools or not. If you cannot share the project information that someone is asking for, say so. Aim for transparency with all your project communications—internal to your organization and externally as well.

Transparency the NASA Way

In *Research-Technology Management Journal*, Jason Crusan, Director for Advanced Exploration Systems at NASA, explains that transparency in projects has to be there during project low points as well as during the high points. In other words, you can't switch transparency on and off: If it's a value your project team is going to have, you have to go all in.

He explains that a NASA project team was testing a next-generation lunar lander. Having gone through a series of test flights, they moved to free flight and on the second attempt, the lunar lander flew, then crashed spectacularly. His team was live streaming the tests and the mainstream news picked up the story within hours.

Crusan says that the agency was very supportive and the team received an "outpouring of support from the public." This, he concludes, was because the team was routinely active on social media and transparent about their projects. Their huge following was cheering for them and helped turn the experience into a positive learning opportunity about how to recover from a failed test phase (Crusan, 2015).

3. Access to data

You can't collaborate if you can't access the information that you need to make decisions or move your tasks forward. It is easier to work together if everyone has the same version of a document and can access the latest report with a couple of clicks.

Social media marketers talk about "content" as being the most important thing in the online world, and it is no different for your project team.

If your collaboration tools don't make it easy to find and access relevant data for decision making, then people won't use them and the tool becomes irrelevant.

They also need to have the skills to be able to search, filter, produce results from, and synthesize the data they find to turn it into something useful. This skill of digital literacy—being able to manipulate online and digital data—is a management skill like any other and can take practice. Failure to develop this skill and make the best use of the available data could ultimately result in project failure or have personal consequences, like redundancy.

4. Connectivity

The right data needs to be available to your team in order for them to work effectively together on problems and projects. But more than that, it needs to be available to them anywhere at any time.

Project teams are often on the road, at client sites, or working from home. Projects don't stop at 5:00 p.m. at the end of the week and pick up again after the weekend, even if no one is in the office during that time. Being connected to your team and the information you need helps project teams work flexibly when the situation demands it.

Connectivity normally comes in the form of online apps or websites—the very collaboration tools that you'll learn more about through this book. You also need a device to access those apps and websites from. In the past, it used to be the case that we would get the latest gadgets at work first—a BlackBerry or a Mac, for example. They would then spill over into our personal lives for home use. That isn't the situation any longer. It is now far more common for new gadgets to be purchased for personal use and then taken into the office, where we expect them to be compatible.

Connectivity used to be limited to a home or office computer, but now individuals can connect via phones, tablets, gaming consoles, and televisions—providing connectivity on the move. This is why it is naïve of companies to think that banning tools like Facebook from office computers is productive. Individuals can access these sites from their personal devices in working hours regardless of corporate policies.

The Internet of Things is putting more and more devices online, such as being able to control the temperature of your house from your phone. We are probably far from developing an app that lets your fridge tell you a new email has arrived from your project sponsor, but the technology is certainly available.

Much of these technological advancements have been made possible by cloud computing. Cloud computing is the delivery of infrastructure, an operating platform, and software delivered over the Internet as a service. You can buy storage space, platforms to build your own applications, or access to software applications. The latter is often called Software as a Service (SaaS) and is the premise for most of the collaboration tools that you may be considering for use with your teams.

The advantage of cloud computing and the SaaS model is that companies don't have to invest in data centers or massive server rooms, and they can avoid the cost of having to buy, host, and maintain software themselves. If your organization gets busier, you pay your cloud computing supplier a bit more money and they scale up the solution for you to cope with the demand. And if business slows, you can scale it back down. It is a flexible way of managing your IT estate, and it's fast. Simply choose your software and vendor, pay the licence fees, and you are ready. No waiting for the IT team to order equipment, install it, and connect it to your local network, which also means lower capital costs of making the investment in new software.

The cost argument is of great value to project managers looking to deploy collaboration tools in their organization. Many enterprise collaboration tools and hosted social media software packages are available through the cloud (i.e., online). The start-up costs are low, and if it doesn't take off, you can just cancel your subscription. You won't be left tied in to ongoing contracts or with expensive servers sitting idle.

Cloud computing solutions aren't welcomed by everyone. At the time of writing, the general perception is that take-up is increasing, although they are still not the *de facto* way of doing business for many conservative industries. Common issues raised surrounding cloud solutions include:

- Licencing models are often per user. In large companies, this can be a hugely expensive monthly fee that is not offset by the reduction in on-premise server space. This can make a long-term business case difficult.
- As the software is hosted on a server somewhere *not* in your own organization, IT departments and governance specialists often worry about the security of the company's data. Using cloud services means giving up some control, and that can be uncomfortable. Cloud providers can provide security

guarantees, and some will even let you visit their facilities to see the levels of security yourself, which will go some way in alleviating these concerns.

- Cloud computing solutions have also been criticized for not being "green." They are energy-hungry server farms with a high carbon footprint. If this is a concern for you and your organization, research the hosting company fully before committing to doing business with them.

The cloud is used for all kinds of applications alongside enterprise collaboration tools. We won't be discussing cloud computing concepts in great detail in this book, but we will look more closely at dealing with security concerns in Chapter 12.

Technology for Collaboration

All social media tools, including enterprise collaboration tools, are built on the premise that they create a community; members of that community can communicate within defined parameters, data can be shared with the right people, and that data is accessible from anywhere with an Internet connection.

Together, that makes collaborative teams possible. Darren Barefoot and Julie Szabo, in their book, *Friends with Benefits*, describe it like this:

> Collaboration has become a Web 2.0 cornerstone, in part because it endorses the many-to-many model valued so highly by the content creators who live there. Working together online has done a lot to break down the Web's reputation as a hostile, unfriendly, and unsympathetic place. Collaboration assumes trust and good faith, and the Web is full of examples where people bring the very best of themselves to a project, whether raising money online to help fight cancer or making research available for free to anyone who needs it. (Barefoot & Szabo, 2010)

The technology available online has made it possible to work across time zones, languages, and with people you have never met. Becoming closer to those project team members despite them being geographically miles away is a benefit for project managers.

What is Web 2.0?

Web 2.0 is the term given to the way the use of the Internet has evolved to help users communicate and collaborate online. The Internet is no longer full of static brochure-ware sites, but is a rich web of interactive pages that allow us to manage online conversations.

In fact, today we are some way on from Web 2.0. For example, I would argue that the massive impact of Google lowering the rankings of mobile-unfriendly sites, which caused a huge redesign effort across the web in 2015, has stepped us on further than the original Web 2.0 ever imagined. However, this term is still around.

Thomas P. Wise defines what makes a virtual team in his book, *Trust in Virtual Teams*, and while location plays a part, it is not the only factor.

Many teams choose to work virtually even though they are colocated. Think of the teams you know that prefer to use email, instant messaging, or collaboration tools over a face-to-face chat. Today, virtuality is defined by an attitude to work rather than geography. Wise breaks this down into the three factors described below and in Figure 2.1 (Wise, 2013).

Virtual Factor 1: Geography

The more time you spend working with your team in the same location, the less you have to rely on electronic emails and other types of computer-mediated communication, so the less "virtual" your team is.

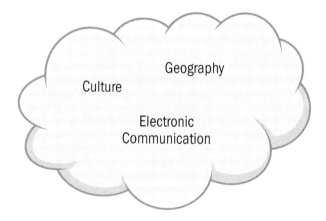

Figure 2.1:   The three factors that define a virtual team.

Geography also plays a part in how well a virtual team bonds at the beginning of the project. The more experience individuals have with working in a virtual team, the better they tend to be at it and at starting off from a trusting position which helps build the team quickly. Wise says that offshore outsourcing companies that only work in this way tend to be very good at hitting the ground running because they have a lot of experience with teams where the members are not in the same location. They assume trust and they assume ways of working that automatically suit the virtual model, whereas team members who have not had prior experience of virtual teams will need a bit of time to find their feet with this new approach. Geographic distance can also mean that conflict manifests itself in different ways. This is something that project managers should look out for, as it can be harder to spot. By the time you realize that there is a problem, it could be a much larger issue than if you had noticed two colleagues having an argument in a project team meeting in your office.

Virtual Factor 2: Electronic Communication

"Virtuality is found in how team members work, not in where team members work," Wise writes. "Communication is often considered to be an indicator of team virtuality." Wise reports that about 70% of people say that over half their communications on projects are electronic. This equates to a lot of teams physically located together who are using a "virtual team" approach.

Virtual Factor 3: Culture

Culture is a factor for every team, and project managers work hard to create working cultures that support successful delivery. Diversity, location, and technical literacy make up part of your team's culture. Your approach to conflict is also a factor in building a team culture. Wise comments that conflict can arise as a result of culture on a virtual team because people don't perceive themselves to be equal, or find it harder to see equal behavior on a virtual team.

Differences in organizational culture (not national culture) are more likely to cause problems on teams and interfere with knowledge sharing.[1]

---

[1] For more on this, see Solli-Saether, H., Karlsen, J. T., & van Oorschot, K. (2015). Strategic and cultural misalignment: Knowledge sharing barriers in project networks. *Project Management Journal*, 46(3), 49–60.

The Limitations of Online Collaboration

It's important to be aware that technology will not necessarily solve or improve issues of communication in the team. If your team members do not trust each other, do not want to work together, and will not share information, making them do those things via an online tool is not going to improve the performance of the project or their working relationships.

Digital technologies can make it easier to communicate, but they still rely on the individuals involved wanting to work together—or at least being prepared to give it a go. If you have the more fundamental issues of a failing team, don't labor under the impression that slapping a collaboration tool into the mix will resolve your team's problems.

Summary

This chapter has looked at a brief history of collaboration and the rise of online communication. Social media tools provide an instinctive way of communicating and getting things done, as humans are naturally predisposed to network and work together.

This chapter has also attempted to define the component parts of collaboration in a project team environment within the context of online tools, namely:

- A sense of community and trust in that community
- Effective communication
- Access to relevant data for making decisions and reporting
- Ability to access data and expertise from anywhere at any time

Technology-enabled communication and collaboration is not limited to geographically dispersed teams. Even colocated teams can work in virtual ways by shifting their communications online and choosing collaboration tools for their projects.

CHAPTER 3

Collaboration Tools 101

Your company probably has a presence on Facebook, Twitter, LinkedIn, YouTube, and maybe even Pinterest, Instagram, or a blog. Today, you'd be hard pressed to find a marketing manager who didn't believe that social media is a good way to engage and connect with customers. They share photos of products on Facebook fan pages. They send out updates and run contests through Twitter. Social media marketing is a recognized way to build brand loyalty, gain repeat business, and encourage customers to spread the word about their products.

Wouldn't you like a loyal, engaged, and committed project team? Let's look at how we can translate the tools and concepts used by marketers for use by project teams.

Collaboration tools are software solutions that are designed to help manage teams and get the job done. They tend to encourage storing all project information, contacts, documents, and discussion in one place, or have the ability to pull in feeds from elsewhere as required. Consequently, the software becomes the main place for project team members to go for updates on tasks and to work with other people.

They are designed to encourage project team members to work together, which can bring efficiency benefits.

Note: Many project management collaboration tools are subscription services using the Software-as-a-Service model. That means there is nothing to download, install, or host at your company. While most of this book is focused on web-hosted subscription services like this, there are still collaboration tools available to install behind your company's firewall (on premises). There are advantages to working this way as well, not least that you don't have to worry at all about security or data sharing. In Chapter 9, we'll look at how you can choose the best tool for your environment.

Collaboration tools have a lot to offer project managers and teams. This chapter looks at the main features of collaboration tools.

They are:

1. Instant messaging—real time chat
2. File upload—docs, images
3. File versioning and collaboration
4. Create groups/teams
5. Share updates
6. Search
7. Reports
8. Workflows
9. Notifications and alerts
10. Liking and gamification

You can find these features either in a bespoke collaboration tool, such as Yammer (part of the Microsoft suite), or as a subset of features within online project management software. Project management software will also have everything you would expect to be able to manage projects such as:

- Scheduling and task lists
- Gantt charts
- Budgeting and expense management
- Resource allocation
- Time tracking
- Dashboards

We won't be covering the features of good project management software in this book, so let's take a deeper look at the collaboration features that will help your team work more effectively.

1. Instant Messaging

Instant messaging (also known as "chat") is a way of sending short text messages to colleagues through the computer. It is similar to email, but faster and with shorter messages. A better analogy would be like having a conversation with someone via text message (SMS), although, again, the results are faster; as fast as you and your colleague can type.

You can normally see a list of colleagues and their status and whether they are available to message or not, which saves you from contacting someone who is not there. This is called "presence" and can extend to other types of technologies as well, for example, showing you whether someone is available to connect over the phone at that time. While you can type a message for someone who is not at their desk in anticipation of them picking it up later, the real value is in synchronous communication where you chat in real time.

There are many proprietary instant messaging applications built into existing software. Talk to your IT department, as it might already be installed. It could be as easy as setting up an account or getting it activated.

Why should I use this feature?

Instant messaging is a more conversational way to communicate with your team than email. It is good for instant status updates when you are up against a deadline, or when things are constantly changing.

Workplace use of messaging tools is catching on widely, and there is great potential in being able to see when your colleagues are online and available to talk. If you can see that someone does not want to be disturbed, you can address your question to someone who is available to chat.

Pros

- Messaging helps you get instant answers to questions. On one conference call, I asked a question of a supplier. He messaged an online colleague overseas who replied with the answer before the call was finished. Without messaging technology, we would have had to wait for a response to an email to get the answer we needed.
- Messaging is direct and fast.
- Many people are used to using this technology at home through Facebook, WhatsApp, Skype, and other personal social media tools. Your team will find the feature intuitive and useful, as they already have experience using it outside of work.

Instant Messaging in Action

Cornelius Fichtner, PMP, was working on a project to build a new home page for a business-to-consumer website. The project had a "war room" in Atlanta, Georgia, which was the base for the team.

"We had to integrate our system with a number of vendor systems," says Fichtner. "We were implementing the latest version of our own software which turned out to have a few 'issues'. The customer, some of the vendors, and our team were all situated in this room working away on various aspects of the implementation. We had development, system analysis, and project management activities going on at the same time."

Fichtner's team was using ICQ to communicate between themselves, which was a popular chat client at the time. "The two developers on my team, myself, and the core system development team back in Switzerland were constantly exchanging information about the latest status of our software," explains Fichtner. With most of the team in the same room, it would have been equally as easy to speak to each other, but with the client and other vendors in the *same* room, instant messaging provided a private way to communicate.

"Discussing the problems in the open would have alerted the customer and the other vendors to the fact that we were having issues with our core system," says Fichtner. "We instantly began chatting about the exact nature of the problems. We determined what needed to be done to put in place instant fixes so that the website code would work and how much time a complete rewrite of the website code would take—which we estimated would be all night long."

Using instant messaging meant that these discussions were held away from the client: It was not necessary to create a reason to have a development-team-only meeting or to worry the client with issues that would be easily resolved. "The chat allowed us to speak to each other in these closed quarters without alerting everyone at the table to the problems," says Fichtner. "That way we could devise a strategy to fix it. The two developers worked all night in the hotel room to rewrite the code for the customer's website."

The incident also served to bring the project team closer together. Looking back, it was a comedy moment in the project life cycle, although it probably didn't feel like that at the time. "For me, the humor was more in the sound effects," says Fichtner. "First you heard the 'normal' keyboard tapping that you hear during code development. Then the chat message, 'The code isn't working' came in, after which the intensity, loudness, and tempo of our keystrokes went up by at least 300%."

Cons

- You have to rely on your colleagues to update their status when they are at their desk. Many of them may prefer to set their status to "busy" which implies they are not available to contact via messaging although they would probably respond to a phone call. The success of instant messaging relies on the individuals being prepared to use it in an appropriate way.
- Messaging is not a good way of generally chatting, as you would do before a meeting or at the water cooler.
- Having your computer "ping" when you have a new instant message can be very distracting. The effective use of this feature relies on good discipline and setting boundaries.
- The ability to get instant status updates can prompt some project managers to go into micromanagement mode. Just because you can get the latest progress on a task every half an hour doesn't mean that you should.

If you are still not convinced about the value of messaging as a tool, consider that Facebook acquired the messaging app, WhatsApp, in February 2014 for an incredible US$19 billion.

2. File Upload

Collaboration tools offer the functionality to upload and share documents and images. You can upload various types of files from meeting minutes, wireframes, or other design documents, and even video and audio. Wikis offer the same features and extend this by enabling the creation of documents as web pages within the tool itself. Wikis will be discussed in more detail in Chapter 10.

The tool becomes the go-to place for storing and archiving project files, which means that everything the team needs to access is in one central location. Files can be organized in folders, by date, or by category. You can see who uploaded it and when.

Why should I use this feature?

File upload features remove the need to keep emails with large attachments or to set up shared folders on your company's network and then manage the permissions associated with them.

Pros

- The project team knows where to look for files.
- You can grant access to external parties like contractors or suppliers more easily than you could with internal server access for documents.
- Search can help you retrieve documents and even search inside documents for key phrases—a great feature when you are looking through an archived project for lessons learned.

Cons

- The file structure needs to be set up intuitively so that it's easy to find the files later. Too many files uploaded with no thought given to the organization will make it impossible to find the relevant documents later.
- People will probably still keep copies of important documents in their email inbox or their personal network drive anyway. It's hard to change habits sometimes.

Sharing and Standardizing with Huddle

"When I joined Cedar, there was no formal policy on where to store project collateral," says Simon Hird, Managing Consultant at Cedar Consulting Ltd in the UK. "There were several shared drives in the organization, but with no owners, and nobody seemed to know what was where or how up-to-date it was. This resulted in a culture of keeping all work on individuals' laptop hard drives, which presents several issues, the lack of ability to share collateral and learnings from engagements and the risk of hard disk failure being just two of them."

Simon had used Microsoft SharePoint with other employers and saw the need to put a knowledge-sharing platform in place at Cedar. He found out that while there was broad support for this, initiatives had been started in the past, but never got past the investigation stage. He proposed an internal project to the company's directors and it was approved with a formal terms of reference and project team.

"We looked at several products including SharePoint. I had read about Huddle in the newspaper and started to investigate that," Simon says. "We mapped them all against selection criteria, and Huddle met nearly all of our needs, was cost effective, and required very little maintenance."

Together with a colleague, Simon designed a project directory structure with sections for Project Management, Functional, Technical, Training, Testing, Upgrade, and so on with subfolders for each, against which the teams could build templates to quickly duplicate standard structures for all Cedar delivery projects. "The adoption of a common folder structure within the project work spaces has been a huge benefit and has allowed all newcomers to a project to find collateral in a consistent manner," Simon adds.

Cedar, a specialist provider of Oracle HCM Cloud (Fusion and Taleo), ERP Cloud, and PeopleSoft services with a 20-year history of delivering projects globally, uses Huddle for the secure storage for company financial records, HR records, policies, and marketing materials. It also serves as a collaboration area for staff to share working and issued documents related to delivery projects, support projects, bids, and more.

"Communication with offshore teams is always an issue, either due to language constraints or geographical distance and time zones," explains Simon. "We use Huddle for several activities during an engagement, such as sharing design documentation and technical specifications. This has meant that everyone has access to the latest versions of documents as soon as they have been updated so there is no longer a risk of an offshore colleague working to an old version of a specification."

It has also saved the team time for other, more mundane tasks, such as storing weekly time sheets so these don't have to be emailed.

"We would absolutely not go back to working without it," says Simon. "If we did not have it, we would need to get a replacement system to replicate what it does. It is vital for a small company where knowledge collateral is so valuable to allow us to easily share it. It has proved invaluable for certain large bids where contributors to certain sections, selected due to their different specialisms, have been able to access required information and then store their responses centrally, irrespective of their time zone or geography. One bid involved experts from Australia, India, Switzerland, as well as the UK, and we could all contribute easily."

Huddle has also been rolled out to the support team which uses a different system that is customer-facing for ticket management. Within that, the support team can store documents such as service level agreements and support manuals, so Simon and the wider Cedar team have to take care not to try to use both systems for the same thing. Huddle is for internal use.

"Share areas are all very well, but are generally unmanaged, get into disrepair, and eventually get forgotten," says Simon. "Using a collaboration system such as Huddle clearly defines who 'owns' documents and who should have access to them. It has been a huge benefit to the business and has been key to our journey toward obtaining ISO9001 certification."

3. File versioning and collaboration

An important software feature is the ability to store multiple versions of the same document. This shows the evolution of the document and is particularly useful if you have an approved, signed-off document that is then amended and reissued. The software will show the different versions and allow you to restore or view a previous version if necessary.

Document collaboration enables the team to work on a document together. You can incorporate your changes or notes and then save them for others to look at. If you are in the process of editing a document, then you can block other people from making changes so that you don't end up with conflicting versions.

Manual version control is time consuming and requires the project manager or configuration librarian to keep a log of all versions, reissuing the latest to each stakeholder every time there is a change. Software-driven version control automates all this for you.

Why should I use this feature?

It's essential that your team is all working from the latest version of documents. Out-of-date requirements, for example, can result in rework and additional project costs.

Pros

- There is no need to rely on your team to remember to update the version number when it makes changes to a document, or for you to be the sole guardian of making approved changes.
- A more streamlined editing process for documents, allowing more people to contribute in less time.
- Everyone always has access the correct version of the file.
- You can see the changes that have been made (and undo them if necessary).

Cons

- Online document storage is going to feel alien to people who are used to using shared network drives or storing files locally on their laptop. This is a cultural shift that needs to be managed.

4. Create groups/teams

Online collaboration tools draw from social network tools to enable you to build your own project network. You can create groups and teams, often including external third parties. These groups then have privileged access to your project files and data.

You can also set up your own profile, as can members of the team. This can include a photograph, contact details, special interests, role in the project, time zone, location, languages spoken, or any other points that you think would be relevant to share with your colleagues.

It's normally possible to brand your collaboration tools beyond individual profiles to incorporate the company logo and colors.

Why should I use this feature?

Groups and teams within the tool allow you to segment projects and initiatives. You can then target communication and updates to the relevant people. You'll also need resource profiles created for your team members if you want to be able to delegate work and assign tasks to them.

Pros

- Everything to do with your project is kept separate from other discussions by only broadcasting to your team.
- Having several teams or groups allows you granularity of conversation while ensuring the people who are interested are involved.
- Using a photo of yourself on your profile helps others in the team put a face to the name, especially when you work virtually with colleagues overseas or in other offices.
- Your team list forms an instant, relevant phone directory that also includes other contact details. This saves you time searching for the last email they sent to pick up their details from the email signature.

Cons

- Your team may well see this as yet another social networking profile to keep up-to-date.
- Watch out for cartoon-style profile photos or other inappropriate images: Remind your team about the professional standards they are expected to adhere to when using the tool.
- Team members may refrain from populating their profile fully, concerned that if they market themselves as an expert in their subject then they will be bombarded by requests for information from other users.
- People need to be added into groups and then deleted from them when their role changes. If they are not removed, they will have access to sensitive project information that is not appropriate for them to see anymore.

5. Share updates

Sharing status updates is probably one of the most useful features of social and collaboration tools. Project managers need to receive information frequently about task progress, and status updates are a good way to do that. They are also useful for messages that need to go to the whole team or for asking questions, for example, when the team needs to have a general discussion.

You can subscribe to updates or topics so that you receive notifications when there are new contributions to the discussion.

Some tools have the ability to send private messages. This would replace an email in this situation while keeping the conversation archived with the rest of the project information in the system.

Why should I use this feature?

Status updates are good for keeping a record of what has gone on, and of course, updating each other informally on progress. You can keep your team on the same page through short, continuous status updates. They can supplement, or in some cases, replace, formal project reports.

Pros

- It keeps team communications and conversations out of your email inbox.
- You can turn status updates into new tasks from the same tool.
- Updates or questions about tasks can be linked to the task and not held as a separate thread.
- You never know when something that someone else is working on will spark a good idea in a colleague (or yourself). The principle of open, transparent communication can build trust within the team and prompt efficiencies that you didn't expect.

Cons

- Making the shift away from working via email can be a challenge for some people.
- Not everyone will "get" the fact that their messages are available for the rest of the team to see. This change to working practices may take some time to embed, as with any change in technology, and require training.
- Management may see the discussion features as a time waster, especially if you ditch status reports in exchange for real-time task updates.

6. Search

Collaboration tools seem great to begin with—a vast desert of empty space to fill with your ideas and projects. In six months, they start to look cluttered. In 18 months, it becomes impossible to find anything. If you are managing a project with a long duration, then you'll definitely find the search feature useful.

Why should I use this feature?

You'll find files that you had forgotten! You'll also save time searching for important records.

Pros

- With everything in one place, a powerful search can trawl through your project data and return the most relevant results.
- It saves you time locating information.
- You can search for people as well as documents, and some tools give you the option to search inside documents, as well. This is helpful if you know what the file is about, but can't remember what it is called.

Cons

- You shouldn't rely on a good search to take the place of decent system housekeeping. Delete old files. Use categories and keywords when you store files so that you have a better chance of retrieving them. Try to create an intuitive document storage system that won't rely on search in the longer term to find anything.
- No search is perfect. You may find that your system doesn't return the records you expect.

7. Reports

Every project needs reports. Project managers use them to track progress against the plan and also for communication. Collaboration tools are no different.

It's worth finding out what reports come as standard with your tool and then thinking about what else you may find relevant. Make the distinction between reports related to managing your project such as a summary of resource allocation on tasks and reports related to using the collaboration tool.

Why should I use this feature?

If measuring take-up and return on investment is important to you, then you'll want to see how the tool is being used. Reports can present the data you need to make informed decisions about where to take the system next.

Pros

- Reports enable you to see metrics, such as:
  - How many messages posted over a given time period
  - Activity from your team or group
  - Member engagement (i.e., how active each team member is on the tool)
  - Number of files uploaded
  - How the members are accessing the product: desktop, via an app, mobile browser, and so forth
- These metrics help you decide whether the deployment has been a success and also to pinpoint areas that might need more support or encouragement to get the best out of them.

Cons

- Many businesses don't routinely assess the return on investment of other communication and collaboration tools. Therefore, these metrics may be of less value than you first thought.
- Data is only valuable if you do something with it. It takes effort to construct a set of meaningful metrics that will deliver data you can work with.
- Your collaboration tool may not come with out-of-the-box reports, which means you will have to build bespoke reports if they are important to you. This often means exporting the data into another tool to manipulate it.

8. Workflows

Workflows are processes with built-in automation. Most commonly, you'll see this with document approval. The document is written, and the author sends it via the workflow to the approver. The approver will then see that this task is waiting for action, either in a system home page or via a dashboard, or through an email alert. The approver will then review and approve the document. When approved, the next step in the workflow lets the author know the document has been signed off on.

Project management collaboration tools may have project-related workflows such as change approval built in. Other tools may have the features to configure the workflow, but expect you to design the process.

Workflows can be incredibly useful when it comes to process efficiency, but that only happens when you have spent the time setting them up correctly in the first place.

Why should I use this feature?

Workflows automate the administration of moving files between individuals. This frees up your time for more value-add work such as leading the team. They can be used for other processes also, such as the change approval process.

Pros

- There is less of a chance that tasks will be overlooked, because they will appear in someone's queue until they are done.
- They save time.
- Alerts prompt action: You'll get better results with an email notification than dropping someone an email yourself.

Cons

- If the standard, out-of-the-box workflows don't work for you, you'll have to build new ones and this can be time consuming.
- The standard workflows probably won't work for you as every organization is different. Technology should support your processes, not dictate them.
- Workflows need to be constantly kept up-to-date, especially when members of the workflow leave. This is a system administration overhead for someone on the team.

9. Notifications and alerts

I love notifications and alerts, probably because, like many people, I can't fully break the link to email. Notifications offer the best of both worlds—alerts when something happens in the tool with a link to carry out the action inside the tool. Users are not tempted to act outside the tool. Instead, the prompt is to login and continue the discussion there.

Why should I use this feature?

Project team members are busy people and so are your stakeholders. It's easy to overlook the latest discussion. Alerts highlight the fact that there is something new to look at on the system.

Pros

- They are easy to set up and turn off, if you feel that you are getting too many.
- They prompt action.
- They provide a comfort blanket for people who aren't ready to give up on their email inbox.

Cons

- If you use the tool routinely, you'll find the constant ping of email alerts unnecessary, because you'll see the notifications in your system home page anyway.
- If you don't use the tool routinely, you'll find the constant ping of email alerts annoying.
- If you switch off alerts and don't log into the system frequently, you'll never know what is going on.

10. Liking and gamification

Whether it's a task, status update, profile photo, or document, modern collaboration tools give you the option to like or "thumbs up" content. This is gamification.

Gamification is a term that refers to the way users interact with software. It relates to elements of the screen design and user interface that promote engagement by rewarding certain behaviors and motivating team members to contribute. This is where "liking" your colleagues' content comes in: The theory goes that if you share an update that is widely liked, you'll be encouraged to share more of the same. It can foster good participation in the system and deepen tool adoption across teams.

Typical gamification features include:

- Scoreboards: Team members are awarded points for behaviors that you want to encourage, such as answering questions in a forum. Users with high scores may appear on leaderboards.

- Badges: Users can earn icons to display on their profile based on pre-set behaviors, such as creating a workflow, reaching a certain amount of comments, and so on.
- Guided missions: Users work their way through a process. Their progress is displayed in terms of percent complete, with the unspoken motivation being to reach 100%. You'll see this in action in your LinkedIn profile, but it can also be used for guiding people through training programs in a certain order.

Why should I use this feature?

Liking something is a convenient way to tell the recipient that you have received the message. Your likes and favorites are also good ways to create a list of content that you access often. Plus, it can be engaging for the team and drive adoption of your new tool.

Pros

- This can be motivating behavior for some team members and it can encourage them to get on board with using a new tool when it is first implemented.
- It's fast: It takes less than a second to mark something as a favorite or to like something.
- You can see what other people have liked, which draws your attention to files and discussions that you might not have looked at yet.
- You can unlike something easily if you make a mistake or no longer need to track that piece of information in your list of likes.

Cons

- Gamification isn't going to engage everyone. You'll have to look for other ways to encourage participation from team members who are not motivated in this way.
- Gamification can be addictive! I once answered a hundred project management exam questions just to get the badge to say I'd done it. This may take people away from the important tasks related to their project.

Gamification isn't right for everyone

Sahar Kanani, PMP, is Manager of Information Services at Telus, a telecommunications company in Vancouver, British Columbia, Canada. She turned down the opportunity to gamify task management tools to motivate millennial team members.

After looking at the system, which would assign points to individuals for completing certain tasks, she concluded that it didn't fit well with the company culture. "If you're a small startup, it might be a good investment to attract a lot of young developers," Sahar says. "For another type of organization, though, it might not add as much value."[1]

How do collaboration tools compare to social media?

Social media purists would argue that enterprise collaboration tools fall outside of the strict definition of social media. However, as collaboration tools adopt social media-type functionality to support the way that users prefer to work, the boundaries are becoming more and more blurred.

"When it comes to collaboration, social media tools and enterprise social software are very close," says Andrew Filev, CEO and Founder of Wrike. "Wrike is enterprise social software for managing projects and teams, rather than a pure social media tool. I think it's important to distinguish different use cases for social media tools: personal chatter, marketing, collaboration. Enterprise social software usually blends capabilities of social media with features specific for managing teams and businesses, like planning and scheduling features in Wrike's case. This allows managers to keep all the information, otherwise flowing through various channels, in one place."

The Disadvantages of Collaboration Tools

While collaboration tools have many features that are designed to get teams working efficiently and cut down the friction in communication,

---

[1] This case study originally appeared in *PM Network*®. See Merrick, A. (2015, July). Will the latest hot trend bring you real results? *PM Network*. Retrieved 4 August 2015 from http://www.pmi.org/Learning/PM-Network/2015/latest-hot-trend.aspx

it's important to consider the disadvantages as well as the potential benefits. We saw some of these in the "cons" listed above, but it's worth taking a moment to explore the disadvantages in more detail.

Collaboration tools are not as intuitive to use as you might think, so training is normally required to ensure the team gets the most out of any new system. As they have many features, you may find that some (the easiest to use) are used frequently, but that others (the more complex functionality) are not used at all.

Team members need refresher training from time to time and you'll also have to factor in training for new starters. It's an ongoing commitment. As there are so many tools on the market, your new starters may not have experience using the products that you do, even if they have experience working in an environment with collaboration tools. It's not as simple as saying you are a confident and competent user of Microsoft Word or Apple's Pages.

Collaboration tools require corporate investment, and the appetite for this investment might not be there for a fledging social media program.

Finally, collaboration tools are designed to hold everything in one place, but project teams will often find ways of working outside the tool. For example, although their collaboration software has document management capabilities, they may prefer to store their documents on a shared network drive. This negates some of the benefits of using the systems in the first place. It is possible to find a way to blend "old style" working practices with collaboration tools, provided the project manager is aware that it is happening and the team openly looks for ways to make the system—digital, "old tech," and offline—work for them.

Summary

Collaboration tools have a lot of different features, some more useful than others. Knowing what each feature does and how it can support communication and efficient teamwork will ensure you have a good chance of meeting your team's needs and making any system deployment project a success.

Weigh the pros and cons of what your tool can offer so that the focus is on what will really add value to your team.

CHAPTER 4

Communication and the Project Management Life Cycle

You'd be hard pressed to find someone who didn't believe that communication was a critical part of project management. And as we have seen in Chapter 3, a lot of collaboration tools have communication at their heart. Before we talk about how technology can address some of the communication needs on projects, it will be helpful to think about what communication is required during the project management life cycle.

This chapter discusses how communication is used and required during the life cycle, and then goes on to look at the communication challenges for project managers. Finally, we'll look at how collaboration tools can address those challenges and contribute toward excellent project communication at every point in the project's journey.

The Project Management Life Cycle: The Communication View

You communicate all the way through a project, right? So, it might seem strange to view the project management life cycle from the perspective of the communication points through it. However, while communication is a constant throughout the project, *what* you are communicating and *why* you are communicating it does change.

All project management life cycles follow the same broad approach to delivery. The phases each project goes through are:

- The initiation phase, where the idea is scoped into a project and the work is authorized.
- The planning phase, where work is planned and organized in detail, along with the people to do it.
- The delivery phase, where the work is done and which might involve a number of delivery phases, depending on the size and scale of the outputs.
- The closure phase, where the project is brought to an orderly close.

You can see this flow in Figure 4.1. Let's look at each of these phases in detail.

Initiation Phase

During this phase, the project gets started. The project team might not be fully in place, so the key audience for communication during this time is the project manager and the senior stakeholders, normally the project sponsor and the key customer, if they are different. This group will establish what is to be done and how it is to be done, and the communication at this point is likely to be a mix of formal requests for work—for example, a business case or project charter—and informal discussions about how best to get this done.

Communication planning is likely to take place at this time, at least at a high level. It's worth thinking about how you intend to use your

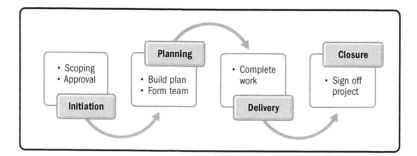

Figure 4.1: The project management life cycle.

digital tools to facilitate communication during the future phases of the project. A key communication need is to enable a "Golden Thread of information which flows from project inception to completion and touches all stakeholders and actors" (Major Projects Association, 2015).

Assuming you've already communicated that the project has been approved, the key messages during this phase are:

- Project benefits: Why are we doing this?
- Project success criteria: How will we know we have done a good job?
- Project organization structure: How will we manage and run this project?

Collaboration tools have a huge part to play in successful communications because they allow everyone access to the same data in real time, or at least the data that they are authorized to access. During the initiation phase, you will be setting up your collaboration tools, and the opportunity to set the tone for ongoing project communications starts then. Consider setting up an area in the project work space or a shared folder for communications materials and key published messages.

Planning Phase

As you'd expect, during the planning phase, the project work is planned. More people get involved at this point too, so your communication net expands as other team members find themselves providing estimates, scoping the work in more detail, and getting involved in the other things required to get the project properly off the ground.

Not everyone who will be affected by the project becomes part of the project team. For example, the very first project I managed completely on my own was to bring a service that had been outsourced in-house. The project went well and on the appropriate day, I gave the go-ahead for all the mail to be redirected to our office, instead of the outsourced office that had been handling it. Overnight, the mail room came to a standstill. Piles of mail mounted up and the staff in the basement struggled to keep on top of it all. I had forgotten to tell the mail room supervisor that this was happening, so she was unable to plan for the influx of extra mail. She and her team were not directly involved in the project—they didn't need to show up to team meetings, and so on—but if I had identified them as stakeholders at this early planning phase, I would have saved everyone a lot of trouble. So, think carefully about who forms your audience for communication at this stage in the project.

The key messages during the planning phase are:

- Project commitment: What is the plan we have signed up for?
- Project team: Who is doing the work?

During the planning phase, your collaboration tools will help you communicate changes and the latest status to the team. Check that everyone has access to the system and if they were a late joiner to the team, get them set up with a username and password.

Delivery Phase(s)

If it is a large project, there are likely to be several delivery phases, bound by significant milestones and an authorization process that moves the project team from one phase to another. If your project environment uses agile concepts, then you may consider these to be your sprints.

Delivery is where the bulk of the project work gets done. Communication at this point is particularly important, because if people don't understand what is expected of them, then they will deliver incorrectly against project tasks. If you have had that experience on a project, you'll know that correcting a mistake once you are fully into delivery is a lot more complicated (and costly) than getting it right the first time.

The communication requirements during these phases are largely dependent on what it is that you are trying to deliver. You will have to involve all the relevant parties—internal and external—to make sure that you give clear direction regarding what project tasks need to be carried out. You'll also get reports back on progress and early warnings of new risks or other problems. Then there is the upward communication to the management team and project sponsor as well, so they are kept up-to-date with progress. Plus, there may be formal reporting requirements to the Project Management Office.

The key messages during the delivery phases are:

- Project deliverables: What tasks are we doing and who is doing them?
- Project progress: How are we performing to schedule/budget?

- Project control: How are we measuring and controlling risks, issues, and quality?
- Project approval: Should we be moving to the next delivery phase based on the current project status?

During the delivery phases, it's essential to keep the project team updated on progress, and collaboration tools can do that. Use the dashboard or project summary pages if available, or set up a personalized dashboard to stream incoming communications.

This is also the phase where you may feel as if the amount of information is overwhelming. There are tips on how to manage the perception of information overload in Chapter 11.

Closure Phase

Once all the work is done, the project has to be closed down in a controlled manner. This allows the project team to evaluate the achievements of the project against the objectives and hand over the operational elements of the project to the key customer.

There's a lot of communication happening in this phase, particularly as you will want to avoid being called on in six months to answer a question about this project when you are in full delivery mode on another initiative.

You'll be communicating with other teams about the lessons learned. Think of it as passing on your project's digital legacy if you've used online tools.

You also communicate the project's success in this phase. This is the point where you send out party invites, or at least say thank you to those who contributed. Of course, that assumes your project was a success and did deliver everything it set out to. If that wasn't the case, there is still cause to say thank you to the people who worked alongside you in getting something done. Projects that close prematurely still need communication and formal close down. There might be something that you can save, and even if there isn't (or *especially* if there isn't), you would do well to spend some time with the project team discussing the rationale behind why the project was shut down and what they personally can take away from the experience.

The key messages during the closure phase are:

- Project evaluation: How did we do against our success criteria and/or other measures?
- Project legacy: What lessons did we learn?

- Project status: Can we confirm the project is now closed?
- Project handover: Who are we handing over to and have they accepted the outputs of the project?
- Project team: What is the project team going to work on next, now that the project is closed?
- Say thank you!

During the closure phase, you can use your collaboration tools to communicate the achievement of the major milestones, but I would strongly advocate for also saying thank you in person. Don't rely on posting a chat message in your project work space as the only and final way you send your appreciation to those who have worked on the team during the project. The messages and audiences for each of the project phases are summarized in Table 4.1.

Table 4.1: Communication messages and audiences throughout the project management life cycle.

Project Phase	Key Messages	Audience
Initiation	• Project benefits: Why are we doing this? • Project success criteria: How will we know we have done a good job? • Project organization structure: How will we manage and run this project?	• Project manager • Project sponsor • Key customer • PMO
Planning	• Project commitment: What is the plan we have signed up for? • Project team: Who is doing the work?	• Project manager • Project team members • Other staff affected by the project • Project sponsor • Key customer • Suppliers/third parties • PMO
Delivery	• Project deliverables: What tasks are we doing and who is doing them? • Project progress: How are we performing to schedule/budget? • Project control: How are we measuring and controlling risks, issues, and quality? • Project approval: Should we be moving to the next delivery phase based on the current project?	• Project manager • Project team members • Other staff affected by the project • Project sponsor • Key customer • Suppliers/third parties • PMO
Closure	• Project evaluation: How did we do against our success criteria and/or other measures? • Project legacy: What lessons did we learn? • Project status: Can we confirm the project is now closed? • Project handover: Who are we handing it over to and have they accepted the outputs of the project? • Project team: What is the project team going to work on next, now that the project is closed? • Say thank you!	• Project manager • Project team members • Other staff affected by the project • Project sponsor • Key customer • Suppliers/third parties • PMO • Wider corporate audience

Communication Challenges for Project Managers (And How You Can Address Them)

Communication is so important for the successful delivery of projects. However, as all experienced project managers know, it's not that easy to get right. There are four main communication challenges facing project managers:

1. Communicating up and out to stakeholders and sponsors
2. Managing miscommunication
3. Communicating for team building
4. Managing the team's communication preferences

Let's take a look at each of those and see how collaboration tools can help address them.

1. Communicating up and out to stakeholders and sponsors

One of the hardest types of communication for project managers is getting the right messages to the right people outside of the immediate project team. Project sponsors are not always as available as you would like them to be, and they don't always have a detailed understanding of what is happening on the project. Messages to project sponsors need to be accurate and informative, but without going into a lot of detail. Sponsors are busy people.

Other stakeholders require different versions of the message. Some may need a lot of detail, but only on certain aspects of the project. Others will only ever want a very high-level progress report. External stakeholders may receive a version of project events that has been sanitized for communicating to third parties.

Managing these different communication requirements can turn into a full-time role, and very few projects have a permanent communications manager. Project managers need to find a way to give out the same strategic project communications without having to rewrite everything from scratch for each individual stakeholder.

Technology makes it easier for stakeholders to control the type of communication they receive. They can set up alerts from your project work space if they want real-time information, or you can configure a personal dashboard for them that highlights the metrics they really care about. Core stakeholders can then access the tools whenever they want, as long as you have set up a login for them and managed their account permissions so they only see relevant data.

Just be aware that alerts and dashboards are only helpful in communicating if your stakeholders use them. Many stakeholders, especially sponsors, like to have access to collaboration tools for purposes of transparency, but won't actively use them to get progress information. You may still have to push information to stakeholders through standard project management reports. This report format can be a snapshot of a dashboard as a PDF file or even a screenshot, but it ensures they get the information you want them to have.

Stakeholders also have a greater degree of flexibility when it comes to how they receive project information. Collaboration tools have a high degree of compatibility with mobile devices like phones and tablets. Many also have apps, which provide even more options for the team on the move.

2. Managing miscommunication

Untangling a communications mess is my least favorite activity. Each party believes that their version of the truth *is* the truth, and if the communication was a call to action, that they did the right thing. I have seen it happen so often: Someone "hears" that another person should have done something or gave permission for something. And that person swears that they said no such thing.

Sorting out these confusions is a waste of everyone's energy. If work has been done as a result of the mess, the work is probably wasted too, either duplicated or incorrect. Project managers trying to prevent this type of miscommunication often go completely the other way and put everything in writing via email. This can lead to even more misunderstandings, because although you have an audit trail of what was said, without the verbal and visual clues, your message is open to misinterpretation.

Miscommunication on a project can happen for many reasons, and technology will not help fix every instance of someone misunderstanding what someone else has said. However, there are benefits to using collaboration tools that will help eradicate some of the causes of miscommunication. For example:

- Project-based collaboration tools encourage relevant communication, so the conversation is less likely to become distracted. When discussion goes off on a tangent, the original thread becomes lost and team members have less recollection of what was being discussed in the first place. Discussion features in collaboration tools keep the history in a way verbal communications cannot.

- Writing things down improves clarity, as team members think through how to best put their messages. This is particularly relevant with team members who do not share the same first language.
- Enterprise collaboration tools have organizational memory. They keep an archive of all discussions and conversations in a way that is easier to reference than email. This improves record keeping, which makes it easier to clarify decisions and requests later on.
- Putting things in writing takes more thought than blurting out, "You're always the same, you never check the impact of scope changes properly." Collaboration tools can help avoid a blame culture.

Miscommunication is often caused by the speed in which the message is passed. A hasty email or a voicemail can be the start of a long miscommunication. Collaboration tools are also fast ways to communicate, so there is a risk here. Stress to the team that speed of response is useful when it comes to firefighting project issues, but it is the quality of the communication that is more important for a successful project delivery.

Miscommunication in a fast-paced, online environment is easy to spot. Monitor the number of questions asked and keep an eye on what is being discussed and how relevant it is to the task you know needs to be done. By bringing this type of miscommunication into an open forum, you have a better chance (and more eyes available) to spot it and step in to correct any mistakes before the miscommunication creates further problems.

3. Communicating for team building

The role that effective communication plays in creating a cohesive team is often overlooked. This type of communication happens when you get a discussion going, people collaborate, and the group works toward a common goal. It involves communicating to people in groups, which often feels unnatural or impersonal. However, if you communicate with people in silos, you contribute toward keeping people in those silos, which is not helpful for a productive project environment.

Team-building communication is also used to share the vision and high-level project objectives and to foster team spirit.

Communication that sets the direction of the team is very different from a directive, or call to action communication. Project managers tend to find that the "getting things done" type of communication comes naturally, and they have to work harder at the communications required for building a team.

Collaboration tools foster transparency. You may decide to limit access to the tool for security reasons (for example, to third-party partners or because the project is a commercially-sensitive initiative that the organization does not want discussed yet). But in general, online tools foster a type of communication that contributes to building effective teams.

This is particularly important in virtual teams, where you don't have the visual and social cues for quickly creating trusting relationships. Virtual teams are often expected to start performing and delivering at speed. While technology can help bridge the distance for delivery, project managers also need to foster a sense of "team" in the virtual environment.

True teams are not formed overnight. It takes time to build up the trust required to work effectively as a team. Project managers don't always have the time to work on team building; there are milestones to hit and deliverables to deliver. Any helping hand with creating a team environment in a short period of time has to be beneficial.

In general, the more communication there is, the greater the bonds and understanding between team members. Instant messaging is a good example of a tool that provides the ability to have short, quick conversations that contribute to building team bonds. In practice, instant messaging only works when all users are in similar time zones or where the difference is only a few hours.

Collaboration tools work best in a trusting, transparent environment, which is exactly the same sort of environment that builds effective teams. Make the most of the features to encourage team working.

4. Managing the team's communication preferences

You have probably worked with someone who:

- Doesn't check their email
- Doesn't check their voicemail
- Doesn't know how their smartphone works

- Emails in the middle of the night expecting a reply straight away
- Sends emails and then immediately comes over to your desk to ask you the exact same question

All of those behaviors feel frustrating to the person on the receiving end if this is not the way that you work too.

It's no surprise that different people work in different ways. Unfortunately, project managers are the ones that bend to suit the working habits of our teams (except for replying to emails in the middle of the night. Protect your downtime at all costs). There is a certain amount of cajoling we can do to get people to follow project management practices, but if we want the best out of the team, we have to take into account their personal communication preferences.

The first step in being able to accommodate your team's communication preferences is to understand what those preferences are, regardless of whether you go on to use collaboration tools on your project.

Personal communication styles cover a range of different aspects. The easiest way to find out how people prefer to receive communication is to ask them. Here are some starter questions:

- Do you prefer the big picture view or to focus on the details?
- Do you like to hear options or to be told what to do next?
- Do you like to weigh all the pros and cons before taking the next step?
- Do you want to get to the end of the message so you can get on with what needs to be done?
- Do you like to hear that it has worked elsewhere or to check it out yourself?
- Do you "see" what someone says or "feel" that something is happening?
- Do you think in pictures, in lists, or in some other way?

This is by no means an exhaustive list, and I'm sure you can think of many other ways in which people like to receive messages.

Collaboration tools offer the ability to tailor communications for the individual recipient. Team members who travel a lot may prefer to receive text messages to their mobile phones instead of email alerts that they might not be able to pick up until later, for example.

You may not, however, be able to easily accommodate the preference for receiving information visually, for example in a mind map. The majority of enterprise collaboration tools are heavily text-based, but with the option of uploading images and media files. Look for ways of incorporating mind maps, video, photos, screenshots, and other visual tools into your discussions and records. They provide a different dimension for everyone.

While people have inherent preferences for communication, the most important thing to foster is good communication, transparency, and an openness to business change in the widest sense. If you have a choice about who works on your project, pick people who have demonstrated that they can communicate articulately, whatever method or style they naturally gravitate to.

Project managers have managed the communication challenges inherent in projects for years without digital tools. However, those old methods are no longer an acceptable way to manage stakeholder engagement. As we saw in Chapter 2, the way in which people expect to be communicated with has changed as technology has evolved into a more interactive, real-time proposition. Project communications are no exception. On top of that, collaboration tools can alleviate some of the communication challenges that we have just lived with or found long-winded and expensive ways around.

Collaboration tools have communication at their heart, so adopting this type of technology as part of the project management tool kit can provide alternative, streamlined ways of getting your project messages across.

Summary

Communication is an important part of the project management role. Collaboration tools can be used throughout the project as part of the communications plan. You can:

- set up sponsors and stakeholders with bespoke alerts and dashboards for relevant information,
- avoid miscommunication through better quality online discussion,
- use the participative features to foster effective team building, and/or
- store different types of data—text and visual—to accommodate the communication preferences of your team.

CHAPTER 5

Team Management and the Project Management Life Cycle

Projects are done by teams. Occasionally, I have found myself working on something very small, all by myself. But most of the time, project managers lead a team of people working toward a common objective.

Collaboration tools, as we saw in Chapter 3, move work processes online and bring people together in a digital, virtual environment. They can help facilitate the management of groups of people. Before we get to how you can achieve that on your projects, it is worth taking the time to explain what project team management actually looks like during the project management life cycle.

Managing a project team is different than managing other types of teams, not least because project team structures only exist until the objective is achieved. This chapter will also look at the common issues with managing project teams caused and enhanced by their unique nature.

Finally, we'll look at how collaboration tools fit into all this and how they can help you manage your team more effectively.

The Project Management Life Cycle: The Team Management View

Projects are a collective effort. It takes a group of people to deliver most projects because, ultimately, you are delivering business change on a scale that an individual can't achieve alone.

Even if you are the only person working on a project, the outcome will affect other people and you will have to involve them at some point.

All projects start with a clear objective that is shared across the team, and achieving that objective is a team effort. If someone lets the team down, the project misses milestones, tasks are delayed, and the project manager ends up with a whole lot of replanning and explaining to do. Therefore, managing a team is an important skill for a project manager.

However, being a team doesn't just happen. No team works effectively from the very first day they are thrown together. It takes time to build good working relationships with people and establish the trust that makes it possible to lean on each other during the difficult patches. Bruce Tuckman published a theory of team development in 1965 showing that small groups of people working together go through five stages:

1. **Forming**

   In this first stage, the team has only just come together. The group relies on the team leader to set the direction and divide up the work. The aims and objectives of the working group are not yet clear and the team members may have different interpretations of any common goal statement. At this point, the team members may not fully understand their role in achieving the overall objectives or why they have been put in this team at all. The team leader will spend time explaining all this and the strategy for the team. Work is done, but it can be haphazard, with all team members adopting their own processes (or none at all).

2. **Storming**

   The second and, arguably, the most difficult stage of team development is storming—and there is plenty of arguing. The team members and the leader need to establish their positions in the team, so there is the potential for leadership challenges, uncooperative behavior, and little subgroups breaking off to do things "their way." The team is now clearer on what it is supposed to be doing, but relationships between the team members may yet hinder the achievement of that in the most effective way.

3. **Norming**

   The team will segue from storming to norming as they become more comfortable working with each other and within the parameters that have been set. By now, the team leader can facilitate the running of the team, and there is generally agreement among the team members. Everyone understands the roles and responsibilities, which are clear. To the outside observer, the team looks functional—and it is. The team works with consensus and is able to spend some time looking at how they work. There is some delegation from the team leader.

4. **Performing**
   At this point, the team knows what it is doing and why: There's a shared vision and purpose with a focus on achieving goals. Teams at this point are usually very autonomous, and if there are disagreements or conflicts, they are resolved satisfactorily. The team leader is able to delegate work to the team members and have the confidence that they will be able to complete those tasks or ask for help if not. The team is focused on achievement, but now also has the capability to look at how those tasks are achieved and suggest improvements to the process.

5. **Adjourning**
   Tuckman added this last stage into his model about ten years after he had originally come up with the first four. It's particularly relevant for project teams, as this is the stage where the team breaks up. Once the work is complete, the team members can go back to what they were doing before, or on to new things. This often comes with a sense of insecurity: What's going to happen next? There can also be sadness, especially if the team members became very close and will no longer be working together. The team leader has to be sensitive to all this and make the transition from team to no-longer-team as easy as possible for the team members.

Unfortunately, project teams don't have the luxury of a couple of months of "getting to know you" time. In a project environment, teams are expected to start hitting milestones and delivering from the very first kickoff meeting. Project sponsors think you can whiz through forming, solve the problems of storming, and end up norming all within the first project planning workshop. Experienced project managers will know that this is rarely the case.

Knowing how to bring together a group of people and create a high-performing team is a key skill for a project manager. However, what

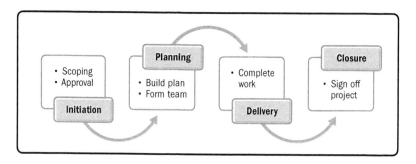

Figure 5.1: The project management life cycle.

"team management" activities you do depends on where you are in the project management life cycle. The way you manage your team on day one is different than how you will manage them halfway through the project or toward the end.

As we did with communication in the previous chapter, let's look at the project management life cycle from the perspective of the team management activities through it. Figure 5.1 shows the project management life cycle diagram again, as a reminder of the four phases.

Initiation Phase

The project is just getting started, so it's unlikely that the whole team is in place at this point. Those who are on the team (the project manager, senior stakeholders, the project sponsor, and the key customer) will have to work together to confirm that there actually is a project to do. This group may not end up being the team that works together daily to deliver the project, but the project manager can still use team management skills to keep the discussions on track and build consensus.

As more people are co-opted on to the team, they will primarily be building relationships with the project manager. This person needs to coordinate the various different groups to ensure that a solid business case or project charter is produced.

Team management activities during the initiation phase are:

- Setting roles and responsibilities, even if some of the team members who will fulfill those roles are not yet in post
- Looking out for team members who you would want to join the project, bearing in mind how the different individuals

would work together. Start thinking about the environment you wish to create. Build a positive work environment by understanding the project's values, culture, and ground rules for collective working; these may change as you bring others on to the team in later phases, but it is beneficial to spend some time thinking about this now.

During this phase, you will set up any collaboration tools that the team will be using during the project. This is likely to include creating a new project work space if the tool is already in use and issuing new team members with their usernames and passwords to access it.

Planning Phase

More people get involved in the project during this phase. The project team members come together. This means that the real effort of team building starts. Up until now, the main relationships will have been between the project manager and each individual team member, which puts a lot of responsibility on the project manager. That means you probably know the individuals better than they know each other, so the team members will come to you for help and guidance instead of going to each other. You have two responsibilities—getting to know the individuals better yourself and enabling them in getting to know their colleagues.

It helps to know what motivates the individual team members, as this gives you information to delegate effectively and facilitate the team working together. How do they like to work? Where do they see themselves in five years? The more you know about their preferences, the easier it will be to work with them in a way that feels natural and avoids conflict as much as possible.

This is also the point to encourage everyone to spend time getting to know each other, and the amount of time this takes should not be underestimated. Build in plenty of downtime during face-to-face meetings so that people can chat. It's not wasted time; it sets up a structure for trust between team members and allows people to start building confident relationships with others.

As the team gets bigger and you bring suppliers or other stakeholders on board, the project manager will not be able to keep individual relationships going with everyone—and you shouldn't have to. In one of my projects, the technical expert managed the relationship with the technical suppliers. He was much better placed to understand what

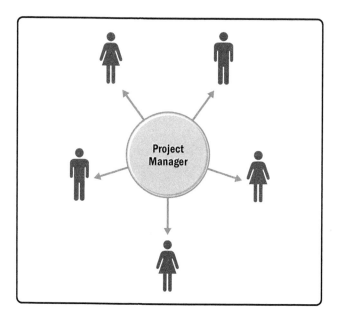

Figure 5.2:   Relationships managed by the project manager.

they were talking about and to coordinate their work on the project than I was. And as the project manager, I didn't have the time to invest in that peripheral relationship, but as I knew and had confidence in the technical expert, I was happy that he was able to take that on. In the end, our project structure looked more like Figure 5.3 than Figure 5.2.

Team management activities during the planning phase are:

- Managing the onboarding of new joiners to the team who were not involved in the initiation phase
- Agreeing to the ground rules you formed in the initiation phase and creating the project culture
- Creating an environment that encourages all the team members to get to know each other
- Confirming roles and responsibilities
- Understanding the personalities and profiles of the people you have on the team
- Building trust and confidence in each other

During the planning phase, you will be using your collaboration tools to work together to establish the tasks. This is a highly interactive phase

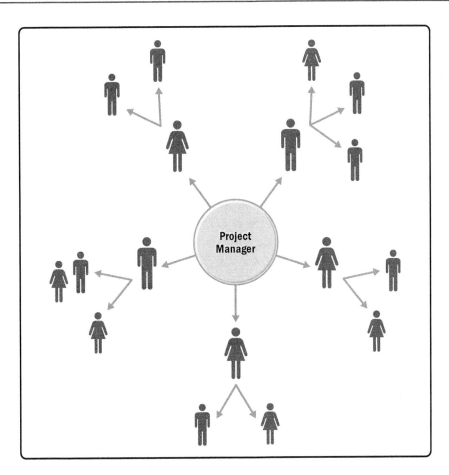

Figure 5.3:   Relationships managed by the project manager and immediate project team.

with the need to keep everyone updated on progress, and with a high pace of change. A system that captures your decisions would be helpful during this phase.

Delivery Phase(s)

Team management during the delivery phases takes on a different feel. By now, you all know each other—at least well enough to get started delivering on the right foot. You'll continue to build those relationships, but there is another focus now—achievement of tasks against the plan.

The project manager will delegate tasks to the team members. In addition, the management activities during these phases of the project are mainly based on giving out work, receiving progress updates, and ensuring everything stays on track. As you know, you can now think about which people on the team you are able to give certain tasks to, because they are the expert or because they would like the development opportunity. There are process considerations to be taken into account here as well, so that you can ensure everyone is doing things in basically the same way. This will make your life much easier.

If the energy of the project team is going to wane, it will be here. During initiation and planning, people will generally be excited about what is going to come and their roles doing something new. The project work could feel repetitive by the time you get through a couple of delivery phases. The shiny newness has worn off and your team members might need some different management techniques to keep them motivated.

There is a big overlap here with communication, as a lot of what you need to do to manage is also about communicating. For example, project status updates will be *communicated* to the team in order for them to better *manage* their own activities.

Team management activities during the delivery phases are:

- Managing task allocation, status reporting, and project progress
- Keeping up the "getting to know" you activities to further cement the team members into a high-performing team
- Monitoring morale and doing something about it if it starts to fall
- Ensuring everyone is aware of progress as well as issues, and how these relate to their own deliverables

During the delivery phases, you will be delegating work, tracking progress, and managing risks, issues, and changes. Collaboration tools will assist with all of these by keeping you in touch with the work of the team, recording key information, and reducing rework by enabling everyone to share common documents and data.

Managing Projects from a Distance

Brett Harned is a digital project management consultant who works with several teams to better their project management practices. He often finds himself working remotely with large teams and is always looking for a tool to help him manage from a distance. He has been using Slack[1] as a central communication platform since the tool hit the market in August 2013.

"Slack has been quite useful when it comes to keeping in touch—and building a rapport—with remote project teams. It helps to build a team environment on projects where that could have been a struggle due to geography," he says.

He and his teams use Slack to communicate in real time about project details and decisions. There have been times when using Slack has allowed the team to come to a consensus on design deliverables and cut down on wasted project time. For instance, on a website redesign project, a designer wanted to share basic sketches for the team to review. She posted the designs in Slack, and the team was able to comment on the files and have a brief discussion about the direction the design was taking. Previously when this was done, it required a meeting of some sort. But with Slack, quick replies with notification of who was typing, as well as emoji responses to comments, cut down on the typical clutter and helped the team get to the point.

As a project manager who is always in meetings or traveling, he enjoys the mobile version of the app. Not only does it mirror the experience on desktop, it's easy to post responses and stay engaged with the team on the fly. The only drawback that he finds about the app is that almost too much conversation happens in Slack. There are times where important project decisions can be made within the tool, and are not communicated to the rest of the team.

"Just as with every other tool we use, we've had to set up some rules for how the team uses Slack—and are sure to share important project information with everyone—in and out of Slack," he said.

Mr. Harned has also found numerous other ways to use Slack. He's been communicating with other project managers in a private account where they share ideas and resources. He also just used Slack at the Digital PM Summit, the conference he organizes. All event attendees, speakers, staff, and volunteers joined the account and organized themselves around topics, activities, and sessions. It was a great compliment to the in-person experience and was proof that many project managers enjoy using Slack.

---

[1] A messaging app for teams, see https://slack.com

Closure Phase

Team management activities in the closure phase are all focused around closing down the project and disbanding the team in a structured way. Your role as a team manager switches from getting the doing done to managing the individuals back into their day jobs or on to another team. This can be a hard part of team management, as you are effectively giving up your team and sending them on their way to other jobs. A new project team might be over the horizon for you, so you have to face the emotions that come with building another team and doing all of that work all over again. Or, if things haven't gone so well, you might be pleased to see them go!

The objective of this phase is to close the project down in a controlled way, so the first team management activity is to make sure that the team understands this change in direction. It's no longer about completing project tasks. Unfortunately, a lot of project closure activities are pretty boring. There's paperwork to complete, user manuals to update, and lessons learned to capture and enter into the organizational repository. All this has to happen against a backdrop of people concerned about their own future or already thinking about their next project or role.

Team management activities during the closure phase are:

- Ensuring lessons learned are captured and passed on
- Marking the disbanding of the team with some kind of celebration or individual acknowledgment
- Managing the transition of the project team into their new roles or back to their day job

During the closure phase, you will be updating records in your collaboration tools to close down open actions, deal with outstanding risks, follow up final conversations, and archive the project's data.

Team Management Challenges

Being able to manage a team is essential to being a great project manager. It's not easy to manage a team, especially when the members don't work directly for you, or when you have to compete with their other commitments. There are four major challenges for managing teams in a project environment:

1. Managing dispersed or virtual teams
2. Managing across cultures

3. Managing part-time team members
4. Managing people who don't work for you

Let's take a look at each of those and see how collaboration tools can help address them.

1. Managing dispersed teams

Teams that are not colocated can present a number of different challenges for a project manager. How will you know that they actually are working on what you want them to? How will you get in touch with them?

Your dispersed or virtual team could also be spread over several time zones. How will you conduct real-time team meetings? Who is going to be the person who gets up in the middle of the night for a call with the Australian development team to go through the testing results? In this situation, and in the absence of incentives for the project team, the project manager will find it difficult to recruit volunteers.

Project managers also have a role to play in protecting the interests of the team back at "base." A project sponsor who doesn't appreciate that you have just spent half the night on a web conference with the manufacturing supplier in Japan will criticize a team that then goes home at 2:00 p.m. Project managers with international responsibilities not only have to educate team members on how to work well together, but also have to manage upward and ensure that senior stakeholders understand the constraints of this type of project. In reality, projects take longer with international teams and involve higher travel costs than projects where the entire team is colocated. And that isn't always a welcome message to the senior team.

Research done by the U.S. Civil Engineering Research Foundation shows that colocation contributes to effective decision making, attention to detail, and helps the team form a partnership. Projects where the team was not based together suffered from poor communication, procurement problems, and lack of direction (CERFDOE, 2004).

In a modern business environment, it is not often possible to have the whole team working in the same locality. Collaboration tools can help address this by providing a virtual team location where everything happens. The project work space can bring people together online, fostering discussion where, previously, the team members would have had to wait for the weekly conference call or just interact one-to-one with others via email.

Instant messaging and web conferencing allow synchronous communication, but asynchronous communication also has its place in building a successful international team. You could opt for something as simple as using a shared online calendar, where team meetings and project milestones are recorded for everyone to see. When you connect from a computer configured to a different time zone, the calendar will automatically show the meeting at the correct time where you are.

Online collaboration tools might improve the situation for dispersed teams, but they don't negate the need for getting together at key points during the project. If your budget will stretch, bring the team together at critical times in the project life cycle to help build the relationships that technology will continue when everyone returns to their locations.

2. Managing across cultures

Even small companies can operate internationally. Outsourcing agreements and partners overseas means that project managers in organizations of any size face the challenges of managing a team made up of different cultures.

National culture plays a big part in how we act, and we can't change that—we can just learn how to make it work for everyone concerned. That can be hard for senior managers to accept. After all, they have got where they are in the organization by working hard and performing well. They expect certain responses to their behavior and when that doesn't materialize, it is easy to put the blame squarely at the door of the person who hasn't reacted as expected.

Involving another country in a project is a wider concern than just finding ways of working with the people involved. The project environment is typically much more complex than a single-country-based project. While I was working in France, my Indian colleagues rang in to tell us they were being sent home after office buildings in Bangalore were damaged: The death of Indian film legend Rajkumar prompted spontaneous violence among mourners on the streets.

Another time, I found it impossible to get to work after strikes about pensions meant more than 90% of high-speed trains were canceled. A project manager leading an international team needs an international view of the different legal and political environments, in order to successfully navigate unforeseen difficulties or changes.

While projects with an international element present a particular challenge, even teams that are all based in the same country could find themselves working across different time zones. And even if you don't have different time zones to contend with, you could still find it difficult to manage a project team split across several locations.

Cultural understanding is not something that can be tackled by a piece of software. It relies on the emotional intelligence of the project manager, his or her leadership skills, adaptability, and ability to inform and train the teams. However, technology still has a role to play.

It is clear that spending some time with your team members overseas is the best way to understand how they work, but getting to know them online before you go (or if budget constraints mean you can't go) will be beneficial. How do they like to work? Where do they work and how do they respond to using the technology? It is likely that you will face the exact same challenges adopting collaboration tools in teams based overseas as those you face in adopting them in your local team.

In multicultural teams, the principles and ground rules governing the use of your collaboration systems become even more important. In some countries, for example, time is a flexible concept. On projects, however, deadlines are set for good reason. When a deadline is a drop-dead date, make sure everyone actually understands the significance of missing it as, for some cultures, milestones are just a guide.

Multicultural teams can also struggle when there is no common language. Choose a language for your app and stick to it. It's not good for the collaborative, team element of shared virtual working to have side conversations happening in another language, when the main language of the tool is English. English-speaking team members will wonder what they are missing out on, and this type of behavior fosters splinter groups within the project team. Instead, encourage those people who are not communicating in their native tongue. Don't penalize them for grammatical or spelling errors—although many people who speak a second (or subsequent) language are grateful to have their mistakes corrected. Check first!

If you choose to have multiple languages in use on your system, then work with native speakers to get the localization right. This is especially relevant for languages with non-Latin characters, as the way the characters display on the screen in the constraints of the software layout is critical for comprehension.

Web conferencing tools or collaborative tools that enable teams to work on the same document often have the ability to record the presentation or meeting. This means they can be played back afterward, which is useful for colleagues who are participating in a meeting not held in their native language so they have another chance to go over any details they missed.

In short, recognize that the people you are working with won't necessarily work in the same way as you, and the people you are working for won't necessarily want the same things. Have an open mind about the challenges of working on cross-cultural projects—this is the first step in being able to address them in a pragmatic way. Use the tools at your disposal to build a framework to manage the differences and reassure everyone in the team that you can develop a realistic way to work together.

3. Managing part-time team members

Projects have a flexible resource pool: You shouldn't have your specialist resource sitting around waiting for something to do. The project environment lends itself well to using part-time people on the project team. Unfortunately, this doesn't always make it easy to manage them.

Part-time team members may have regular hours that they work on the project, for example, every Monday and Tuesday. Alternatively, they might have particular tasks to do, and they work flexibly around those—a task may be programmed to last 16 hours, and they will split those across the week as required. This can make it difficult to schedule regular team meetings and one-to-one meetings with those part-time team members. In the worst case, part-time team members may refuse to participate in meetings, saying that they "are not scheduled to be working then." Or they may have the best intentions, but find that their other responsibilities—the things they do when they are not working on your project—get in the way.

Flexible working is a great thing, but it comes with a degree of responsibility to your work colleagues and it takes great care to manage effectively so that everyone benefits.

Part-time team members are the most flexible resources in your team, and technology offers many flexible ways of communicating with them. Their personal work space or home page will record project activity while they are not working on the project, providing a useful summary of what has happened while they have been busy with other things.

The use of collaboration tools on a project supports the role of part-time team members. They could listen to a recording of a team meeting, or watch the slides and hear the presentation later. However, you will have to decide how appropriate it is for them to do "catch up" reading when they could be spending their time working on delivering their tasks.

4. Managing people who don't work for you

Part-time team members probably don't work for you: They'll be on loan from another manager, and that creates another set of challenges. Your project priorities will be competing with the priorities of their line manager. And this will cause clashes, with the unfortunate team member in the middle.

Even resources who are seconded to your project on a full-time basis could have a different line manager. While they might be "yours" for a set period of time, team members in this situation are likely to have responsibilities to their original team, such as participating in regular team meetings, helping out when their original department is short of staff, and so on. These are moments where you will have to negotiate with their line manager to find the best possible solution.

Whether they are part- or full-time on your project, the people working alongside you have more in their lives than your project. Personal and professional development is often forgotten for those seconded to a project. Project work itself is often seen to be developmental, but someone seconded to you for a long period of time may be missing out on training courses or other developmental activities that their colleagues back in their "home" department are benefiting from. Projects should deliver something to the organization, but as much as possible, they should also deliver something to those participating in it. When the project team doesn't work for you, you have little control over supporting their developmental needs and longer-term career goals.

Collaboration tools make it easier to co-opt experts on to the team and bring them up to speed more quickly, especially if they incorporate an element of social networking or organizational discovery. The system stores a history of the project, which provides a ready-made induction for any new team members. This is relevant whether they are joining the team on a full- or part-time secondment basis, and can also help when you are bringing someone on board for a very short period of time to do a specific activity.

Discussion groups, in-line comments, and wiki pages are also useful tools to bring people together, whether they work directly for you or are part of a completely separate team that has no impact on your project. These tools allow you to gather information from a wider subset of your organizational community if you desire.

If the team members' original departments use collaboration tools, you should encourage links between those and the tools used on your project (ideally you should all be using the same software). This can help create a bridge between the temporary project structure and the department to which the team member will be returning.

Finally, collaboration tools make project work very transparent. You could give system access to the line managers of your project team members. This will enable them to see exactly what their employees are doing on a day-to-day basis, and could encourage them to be more supportive of those people while they are seconded away from their original departments.

LiquidPlanner: Tools in Action

Liz Pearce, CEO at enterprise collaboration software company, Liquid-Planner, says that the company practices what it preaches when it comes to using enterprise collaboration tools to improve project delivery.

"We use LiquidPlanner for every phase of each release: planning, prioritization, creating the specifications, estimation, vetting design, execution, and bug/defect tracking," she says.

The LiquidPlanner teams use their software to organize, manage, and plan everything from individual daily tasks to marketing projects and new software releases. The company has built its business processes in a way that integrates with the principles of enterprise collaboration and now finds that even process tasks have become second nature to the software's users.

For example, every time there is a new request for a software enhancement, or a bug report, the team uses their enterprise collaboration tool to manage that change to project scope. "All new feature requests are created as new items and dropped into our 'Inbox' package, which we process as a team twice a week," she adds. "At that time, we prioritize, assign, and estimate the work—moving through the list in a systematic and organized way that would otherwise be impossible."

The team can also access their project work space even when members are out and about via mobile devices such as tablets and phones.

As of July 2015, Pearce's teams have been using LiquidPlanner for over eight years, and they have a lot of data stored in the tool. "We've built a work space with over 140,000 comments, attached over 35,000 documents, and managed over 39,000 tasks in one shared system," she explains. "Not only is that information archived and organized for our ongoing use, but it's saved us countless hours of switching costs versus using email as a collaborative tool."

Summary

Effective team management skills are key for project managers across all phases of the project management life cycle. Collaboration tools can be used throughout the project as part of the approach for managing the team to address the challenges of:

- managing dispersed and virtual teams through better communication,
- managing multicultural teams with an awareness of differences in ways of working,
- managing part-time team members by using the archiving and documentation features, and
- managing people who do not directly report to you by using technology to build virtual bridges between them and their original teams.

Making It Work

Part 2 covers the practicalities of making the move to online collaboration tools for project management. It examines the need for a strategy before you even begin to research suitable tools, and provides guidance in preparing your team and senior executives for the change required to shift away from current processes.

It looks at the initial setup and ongoing management of the tools you choose, plus how to deal with information overload and the cultural changes that come with increased transparency and easier collaboration.

It includes the following chapters:

- Chapter 6: Strategy First
- Chapter 7: Is Your Team Ready to Work Online?
- Chapter 8: Winning Over Management
- Chapter 9: How to Choose and Use the Right Tools
- Chapter 10: Getting Started With Collaboration Tools: Using Wikis
- Chapter 11: Managing Online Culture Shock: Risk Mitigation Strategies for Collaborating Online
- Chapter 12: Keeping Your Project Data Secure

Strategy First

The goal for using any software, tool, or technique should be to achieve a business objective. By itself, "collaboration" is a weak goal. It makes sense to think that collaboration tools will improve collaboration across your project teams, but that doesn't automatically lead to better project success rates.

A better goal would relate to improved project outcomes. Defining your goals and understanding what you want from a collaboration tool is part of setting a strategy.

In this chapter, we'll look at how you can develop a strategy and define the requirements you need from a tool. This covers the first three boxes in Figure 6.1, which shows the process of getting from strategy to benefits.

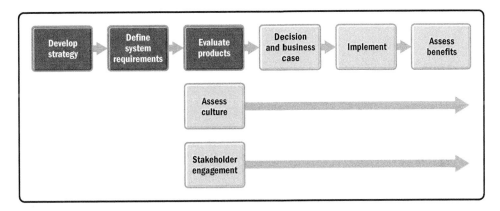

Figure 6.1: From strategy to benefits.

Strategy Before Tools

Before you even start looking at what software solutions might be a good fit for you, it's important to take a step back and consider what problems you are trying to solve.

Your strategy should address the problems facing your project teams and how you intend to overcome these through computer-mediated technology—collaboration tools. Some organizations will expect to see a business case that includes detailed financial predictions, but in many cases that isn't appropriate or necessary. The strategy, and any associated business case for implementing solutions to manage the delivery of that strategy, doesn't have to be complicated.

This short chapter looks at how you can write a strategy and the associated business case.

How Pernod Ricard Did It

In the book, *Leading Digital*, George Westerman, Didier Bonnet, and Andrew McAfee (2014) explain how Pernod Ricard set up an internal company social network. The strategic imperatives to do so were:

- Customers were talking about the company's products on social channels and expecting the brand to engage with them
- Product distributors such as bars were experiencing a digital transformation of their own
- Employees were choosing to use their own social tools in the workplace and expected more from the company
- There was a desire to get the company to communicate openly at scale, across a distributed business model and multiple divisions, some of which were more digitally advanced than others

The objectives for launching an internal network were heavily based on entrepreneurship, innovation, and transforming business practices. The solution chosen enables employees to share data in real time, collaborate from mobile devices, message each other, and act as a global team. The benefits have been improved internal communication including working collaboratively with employees through web conferences to refine new HR practices.[1]

---

[1] For more on this case study, see Westerman, G., Bonnet, D., & McAfee, A. (2014). *Leading digital: Turning technology into business transformation.* (pp. 118–120). Boston, MA: Harvard Business Review Press.

Developing a Strategy

You can prepare your own strategy for adopting collaboration tools with a simple four-step approach.

Step 1: Identify the problems.

The objective of moving to new ways of working should be to address pain points felt by the wider business or specifically by project teams. Think about the kind of collaboration problems that your team is facing, as this will shape the kind of products you assess and ultimately choose.

For example:

- Project delivery teams are perceived to be too slow
- Project teams lack the ability to work together over distance and time zones
- Processes are not standardized or shared
- Project knowledge is not shared, resulting in projects reinventing solutions and templates that other project teams have already created

Make this section as specific as you can. It may help to include input, commentary, or survey results from your team members and the wider project community within your company. This kind of feedback can add weight to your arguments and new angles for the decision makers to consider.

Step 2: Identify stakeholders.

You can't implement a strategy alone. List who is going to be affected by this change in working practices, including:

- Project and program managers
- The PMO
- Project coordinators
- Project team members
- Line managers
- Senior managers who may sponsor any initiatives
- The IT team who may be required to vet any software products before you can use them
- The legal team who may be required to review contracts with software vendors
- Purchasing or the finance team

In addition, identify any new roles that may need to be created or roles that will change in order to take on new responsibilities for delivering this strategy.

Step 3: Define your goals.

Spell out your objectives for new ways of working, including concrete goals for what you want to achieve. Keep your objectives as SMART as possible (specific, measurable, agreed upon, realistic, and timely).

Your objectives should link back to the pain points you have already identified. For example, if project teams are struggling to work in distributed teams, the goal would be for all team members to work effectively together in the pursuit of joint objectives, regardless of distance or time zones. Figure 6.2 shows how these goals link, through strategy, to options appraisal (more on that in Step 4), and your business case (which we'll look at more in Chapter 9) to finally turn into projects that will address your needs.

If you have metrics, slot them in here. In the absence of established and reliable statistical measures, make a note of causal measures or what you expect to see as a result of implementing your vision.

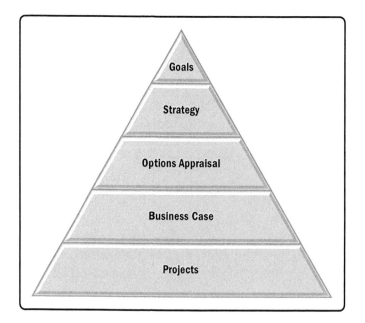

Figure 6.2:   The strategy pyramid.

Your objectives for improving project delivery should align to the wider business strategy, which you'll be able to find in the organization's annual report or vision/mission statements put out by the board. If your organization is one of the 42% that has a digital vision (Westerman et al., 2014), link it to that as well.

Step 4: Identify possible solutions.

This might seem a controversial step in defining a strategy. After all, strategy sets vision and goals, not solutions. However, in practice it's highly probable that during the course of your research and talking to your colleagues, you have come across ideas and products that you'd like to investigate further. Record them, along with your strategy, as a memory jog.

The strategy helps you identify the problems that you want to solve so you can best choose the solution. Sometimes the answer will be technology, other times it won't be. Much process change can be done without technology. In the specific case of project teams, the answer will most likely be a combination of collaboration tools, process change, and cultural change.

Defining What You Want from Your Software

Your strategy should tell you the problems that your teams are facing. In turn, this gives you the information you need to build a list of criteria for selecting a product.

We're going to assess potential software solutions against five elements:

1. Functional requirements
2. Nonfunctional requirements
3. Vendor fit
4. Cost
5. Other strategic elements

The rest of this chapter discusses these elements and shows how you can use them to select the perfect product for you.

Table 6.1 is an example of a software evaluation matrix. Each line item can be rated on a simple, 1–5 scale with 1 being, "meets none of our needs," and 5 being, "fully meets our needs." You can then adjust

Table 6.1   Simple product evaluation matrix for weighting and rating software tools.

Product Evaluation Matrix								
Product Name:			Tool X					
Criteria		Weight	Rating					Total (rating × weight)
			1	2	3	4	5	
Functional Requirements								
	Features:							
1	Document sharing							
1.1	Discussion threads							
1.2	Email alerts							
1.3	Project scheduling							
1.4	Task management							
1.5	Time sheets							
1.6	Wiki pages							
2	User interface							
3	Search							
Nonfunctional Requirements								
4	Access control							
5	Mobility							
6	Interoperability							
7	Configurability							
8	Technical environment							
9	Speed							
10	Accessibility							
11	Legal/Regulatory criteria							
Vendor Fit								
12	Ability to deliver							
13	Financial viability							
14	Flexibility							
15	Other customers							
16	Ongoing support							
17	Exit							
Cost								
18	Value for money							
							Total:	

each result for importance by multiplying it by the weighting factor. This allows you to rate access control more highly than a nice user interface, for example.

You will complete a grid for each product that you go on to evaluate. Totaling the rows and columns will give you a numerical way to objectively compare products against each other.

Don't manipulate the evaluation criteria to get the result you want, but do use your common sense to ensure that your product analysis is giving you the best result. If, when you've completed grids for each product, you feel that the evaluable is giving you the "wrong" answer, then go back to the design of your analysis. Often, gut feel is important for selecting a product. Try to understand why the product you feel attached to isn't the one at the top of your short list. It may be that your evaluation criteria are not evenly balanced. Or they may be perfect and you need to come to terms with the fact that your favorite tool isn't going to make the short list.

1. Functional Requirements

It's tempting to spend loads of time on this area at the expense of all others. This is where choosing a product gets interesting.

However, at this point all you are doing is creating a "feature wish list." You still need to review other product requirements, assess whether your project environment is ready to take on the shift to digital working (Chapter 7), and win over your management team (Chapter 8).

You're a little way off using your list of functional requirements to assess products and choose one.

a. Important Features

First, you'll be looking for a product that addresses all (or the majority) of the pain points you identified as part of your strategy. If your team struggles to find the right version of project files, you'll want version control. If opening the channels for conversation is important, you'll be looking for something with instant messaging or threaded discussions.

Some examples of features are:

- Instant messaging
- Wiki
- Document sharing
- Discussion threads
- Issue tracking
- Email alerts
- Project management functionality (e.g., scheduling and task management)

Pick the areas that are essential for your team. This section will form a large part of your product evaluation and will be weighted heavily.

b. User Interface

An easy-to-use interface does matter. Gone are the days when people preferred functionality over beauty. Today's best tools should be fully functional *and* nice to use. Another benefit of an intuitive interface is that it will save you time training your team.

c. Search

Search is important enough for it to be a functional criterion alone. The volume of data that social tools create makes it essential to be able to find information again, whether it was posted last week or last year. When you use the matrix to evaluate products, ask questions about how easy it is to find documents, other files, discussions, and people.

Ideally, search features should allow you to filter the results by document type/discussion/project/date or other criteria. Without this, you could be returning hundreds of results for "Project Alpha."

Collaboration Tools and Configuration Management

Configuration management is a key element of any project management approach. It is essential that everyone knows that they are working on the latest, approved version of any given document or product. That doesn't change with the introduction of collaboration tools. In fact, computer-mediated communications make good configuration management practices even more important. There is a tendency to think that a collaboration tool means all other project management processes go out the window—that is certainly not the case. Enterprise collaboration tools are there to help you manage a project team and collaborate more effectively, not to replace your project management standards or methodologies.

Establish how you are going to incorporate the products of your online conversations with the existing configuration management processes you have in place. If your new systems will be focused on facilitating communication, then there may not be much need to control those discussions through configuration management. You wouldn't put email through a configuration management process, so why would you do that with discussion threads?

Configuration management does play a part in managing documentation and project artifacts that are shared online. If your project team posts documentation to the project home page or wiki, can you be sure that it is the most up-to-date version? And what happens to people who cannot access that work space or wiki? They still need to be able to access that latest document, which means duplicating it somewhere else—an approach that will not be supported by any configuration librarian.

Avoid clashes with your configuration management system by incorporating your approach into the way you use your collaboration tools. For example, if you know that some of the stakeholders need access to a document, but do not have access to the project wiki, you have two options: Give them access to the wiki, or make the document available elsewhere with a link to it from the wiki.

Enterprise collaboration tools and document management systems normally include a built-in version control feature for online storage of documents. Version control is a way of keeping track of the changes made to a document (or another project management product) over time. Having this functionality built in to an electronic tool mitigates against the risk of failing to remember to update the document number when changes are made. Take advantage of any configuration management features built into your collaboration and document management tools where you can, but ensure that it captures the appropriate level of detail.

Version histories should normally include:

- the version number, incremented by 1 for a major revision, or 0.1 for a minor revision,
- the date of this version,
- who made the changes and who has approved this version,
- who has received copies of this version (the circulation list), and
- the reason for this version and/or a summary of any modifications made.[2]

Double check that your online document repository stores all the previous versions as well as the most recent one. It would be embarrassing to find out that you needed to go back to a previous version, only to find that it has been overwritten.

---

[2] I provide a longer discussion of the role of version control on projects in my book, *Shortcuts to Success: Project Management in the Real World.*

2. Nonfunctional Requirements

Nonfunctional requirements cover your expectations for how the system is going to work. If you have a standard list that you usually use for evaluating the nonfunctional requirements of packaged software, then use that. Otherwise, here are some requirements to get you started, in no particular order.

a. Access Control

How easy is it to add users or remove people who have left? This criterion lets you assess whether individuals can have granular access to files and how easy it will be to grant access to your consultants and third parties.

b. Mobility

Think about how your teams work. Typically, most planning and scheduling is done at a desk while discussion, searching for information, and noting down good ideas can be done online via a mobile solution.

Is there an app that goes with the desktop version that is available for all the operating systems you use such as iOS, Windows, and Android? Can it push out alerts? Is it easy to use with a menu that's designed to help you quickly get to the features you use the most? If your team does a lot of work (or wants to do a lot of work) on tablets and mobile devices, then this criterion will be important to you.

Watch out for software that says it has an app available, but the functionality available through that app is limited. When the time comes to evaluate products, it's safer to check what features are available on the mobile solution instead of relying on the sales pitch. It's also worth checking if the app can be used offline and then syncs back to the cloud version. If not, your project team could find themselves unable to do anything if they lose their mobile signal.

c. Interoperability

Consider what other applications your collaboration tool will have to interact with. At the most basic level, consider how employees will log in. Anything that requires an additional username and password reduces the likelihood that someone will make the effort to use it. Lowering the barrier to use can be achieved by syncing desktop logins with the tool logins (e.g., through the use of single sign-on or Active Directory).

You could also look at whether it is compatible with Google Docs or equivalent for online, collaborative editing. If the product has an application program interface (API), this will help your own IT team develop interfaces between it and other systems, for example, to pull project data into a business data warehouse for analysis.

d. Configurability

Find out how much configuration users can do themselves. Will the tool need a dedicated administrator behind the scenes to make changes, create dashboards, edit fields, or set up workflows? Ideally, you should be able to do all of this without having to ask the IT team to get involved every time.

e. Technical Environment

Make the decision about whether you want the product to be hosted on your own servers, secure behind your firewall, or whether a cloud-based solution is the right move. There might be a hybrid option that would also be adequate for your needs.

If you do need to provide some technical infrastructure yourself, get the right people involved to assess how the tool will work with your existing environment and what additional costs there would be for hardware or operating system licences.

f. Speed

If you have expectations about the speed of response when you click an item or when you save data, then mention them in your evaluation matrix so you can check performance of your short listed products.

g. Accessibility

It's good practice to make sure that the product is capable of being used by everyone on your team, so that means doing some basic checks for accessibility. Color-blind team members may have difficulty with contrasting colors on the screen. Team members with mobility problems may prefer keyboard shortcuts over using a mouse, as they can be used with voice recognition tools.

Think about who is going to be using this product now and in the future and make sure it suits everyone's needs.

h. Legal/Regulatory Criteria

Finally, don't forget to include any legal or regulatory criteria in your product and vendor evaluation. For example:

- Compliance with the U.S. Americans with Disabilities Act, and
- Requirement in the UK to store all public health records within the UK (i.e., personal medical records cannot be stored in a cloud-based system with servers offshore), and so on

3. Vendor Fit

One of the largest risks for companies is to invest in what is effectively an entrepreneurial business. There are many established collaboration tools on the market, but you might want to extend your search to products tailored for your industry or niche, or emerging products that don't have a long history.

It's important to carry out some due diligence to ensure that you are not going to expose your company to financial risk and the loss of data through partnering with a collaboration tool vendor that then goes bust.

Here are some criteria you can use to evaluate the vendor for a good fit with your business.

a. Ability to Deliver

Talk to them about how they are going to deliver the product. What project management and implementation capacity do they have? How do they expect to train your teams and what materials can they provide?

Find out how often they release new functionality and how you will be able to take advantage of this. It's also useful to find out if you'll have the choice to take on new features or not; often, the answer with cloud solutions is no, as developments are done on a platform-wide basis.

b. Financial Viability

Carry out an assessment of the organization's financial health to give yourself confidence that they are a viable business. You want to feel secure in the knowledge that they will still be trading in several years.

As part of this check, you can ask them about using their software under escrow and what would happen if they were unable to support your collaboration tools going forward.

c. Flexibility

This looks at their ability to adapt and respond to changes in the market. This is important if you are looking at a vendor that has a long track record, as you want to be confident they can adapt their software to take into account new trends. For vendors that haven't been around very long, you will want to assess their ability to respond in the future. As you won't be able to gather much evidence of this, you'll have to make a call based on your dealings with them and the impression they give about how connected they are to the market.

d. Their Other Customers

Get references. They should be able to put you in touch with other companies in your industry that are using their products. Find out what their customers think of their product and the service/support that they offer.

You should also check that they are actively marketing their products and have other customers in the pipeline. It is not commercially sensible to contract with a company that is not actively seeking additional work.

e. Ongoing Support

Investigate the support model that they use. Web-based collaboration tools often have online support through a section for frequently asked questions (FAQ). Is that going to be enough? Software-as-a-Service collaboration tools may not be able to give you a dedicated account manager. As the model is predicated on ongoing revenue across a wide user base, getting a named individual to support your business may not happen. Make this a criteria of your selection if you feel you will require it.

f. Exit

Can you get your data out? With the pace of change in the collaboration tools market, it is quite likely that there will be something else that will better suit your needs in five or ten years' time. If that is the case, you will need to extract your project data from this tool and upload it into something else. Or mothball your old tool and make it a "look up" only service for the purposes of audits and knowledge sharing.

Think forward to what your needs might be in the future and how you could meet those needs if they included migrating all your data to another system.

4. Cost

Cost is important. Cost for online tools is often based on how many users you have. What seems cost-effective for a handful of users during a pilot can soon prove to be very expensive when you rack up the costs for the whole enterprise.

Equally, look out for storage costs. In the first year or so, you might not hit your storage limits, but as soon as you tip over into the next level of disc utilization and document storage, then the costs can increase. The number of documents and projects using any tool soon starts to add up once people realize the value and want to move their teams on to the collaboration platform.

5. Other Strategic Elements

There's bound to be something that is important to you, but hasn't made it into this list of requirements. Perhaps 80% of your clients use a particular product and you want to add a criterion for "client fit." Whatever it is, add the requirement to your evaluation matrix so that you have the perfect checklist for your strategy and your business.

The Question of Gamification

As we saw in Chapter 3, gamification is a way of encouraging and motivating employees to use a product based on the desire to connect and "win." It takes the mechanics of games and applies them to a project environment with the objective of increasing engagement by tapping into our innate desire to feel compelled to play. Your desire to participate and progress creates a "pull" that encourages you to continue taking part.

You can gamify non-software project management processes and you probably have over the years. For example, by running a quiz about your project or offering a treat to the team that resolves the most queries by the end of the month or similar. However, gamification in software is now common and relatively easy to implement. You will have seen it, even if you haven't been aware that the software you are using is gamified.

Examples of Gamification

Here are some examples of gamification that you may have already experienced.

- Receiving endorsements for your skills in LinkedIn
- Voting up or down comments on a website
- Clicking to "like" content
- Leaderboards
- Earning points for contributing to forums
- Earning points that move you up the levels, for example, airline loyalty schemes where each level brings more benefits
- Rating articles and having others rate your advice or reviews on websites
- Seeing that your profile on a website is X percent complete

All of these are techniques aimed at getting you to stay on the site and interact more with the site.

Gamification of project management software should encourage participation and the use of your collaboration tools while providing some kind of benefit to the team or organization overall. For example:

- Liking documents will help them appear higher up the search results when others look for them
- Earning badges or points for successfully completing a project checklist for a particular stage or phase with no rework required
- Voting on solutions (although note that you do not have to accept the most popular vote—your workplace does not have to be a true democracy at all times)

Common to most forms of gamification is a visual element. This could be a thermometer showing progress against a target, a leaderboard, badges, or levels shown against an individual's profile or some other form of dashboard. This allows people to see their own progress and that of others, so that they can compare and continue to engage.

If you feel that this functionality would help you meet your strategic objectives through increased employee participation in a tool, then by all means include it in your product evaluation matrix as a functional requirement.

Summary

Strategy doesn't have to be difficult: It's only a prompt to start looking at the problems facing the team before diving into investigating the technology. With your strategy in place, you can start to explain the benefits of enterprise collaboration tools as options for your project management tool kit.

This chapter has looked at how you can kickstart your internal strategy for collaboration tools in a project environment. It has also covered the criteria for evaluating a software product against your strategy, namely:

1. Functional requirements
2. Nonfunctional requirements
3. Vendor fit
4. Cost
5. Other strategic elements

Use these lists as a guide for your own evaluation matrix.

The next chapter considers the change management that needs to sit alongside the deployment of any collaboration tool.

Is Your Team Ready to Work Online?

Now that you have a strategy, it's time to think about how you can meet your strategic objectives through the deployment of a technology system. Actually, wait a moment. First, let's assess whether your team is actually ready to make the shift to using technology-mediated communication.

Using collaboration tools can feel like a very different working environment than what you had before, so it's worth carrying out an "as is" assessment of your workplace prior to making any investment decisions. This ensures that the groundwork is done before a new system is implemented and lets you plan any preparation tasks in terms of team and change readiness.

This chapter looks at the people side of planning to use collaboration tools. Figure 7.1 shows you where we are now on the journey from strategy to benefits—it's the "assess culture" box. This work can be carried out in parallel to your product evaluation and the stakeholder engagement tasks we'll discuss in Chapter 8.

Four Dependencies for a Successful Deployment

There's a solid strategy for using project collaboration tools and a clear road map of where the organization wants to be in the future. Before you start Googling collaboration tools and signing up for free trials, let's take a step back. Is your team really ready to change the way they work and support your strategy? And if not, how are you going to help them get there so you can realize the benefits of adopting online collaboration methods?

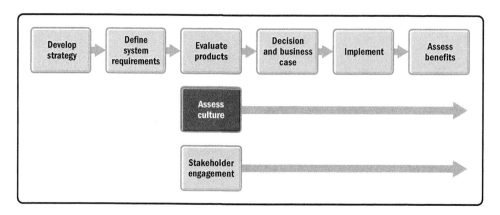

Figure 7.1:   From strategy to benefits.

The following sections will address what considerations you should take into account before launching a new collaboration tool. They will look at the four dependencies for success:

1. Team culture
2. Project culture
3. Organizational culture
4. Personal culture of the project manager

These are shown in Figure 7.2, which explains the readiness factors to consider for a successful deployment of social collaboration technologies at work.

Team Culture: Is Your Team Ready?

The first dependency to consider for your collaboration project is how much your team will want to participate in this. Web-based collaboration tools rely on people being online and willing to share their knowledge, as well as a commitment to cultural change within the team. Ask yourself the following questions:

- How technically literate are your team members?
- Where are they based?
- How keen are they to try something new?

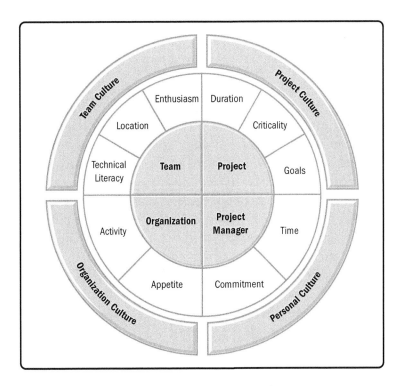

Figure 7.2:   Social and collaborative readiness factors.

A team already confident in using social media and online tools (in or outside the office) will make for an easier adoption of any such technology in the workplace. If you are working with a group of people who struggle to send emails, don't text, and can't use the calendar feature on their mobile device, you could find yourself meeting a technical challenge.

Of course, not being technically savvy is not a barrier to adopting new technology. Collaboration tools are simple to learn; they are designed to be intuitive. However, people have to *want* to learn them.

Email is so popular as a communication tool because there are so few barriers to its use. You don't have to use the same messaging client as the other person. Communication is virtually instant. There is very little technical friction or challenge with email, and certainly less than you'd find with a new collaboration tool. Overcoming email reliance is, therefore, a challenge with any new communication software, and understanding personal motivation and benefits for having to make that change will be critical for you to drive adoption.

People tend to learn new computer skills for a variety of reasons, and as the project manager, you probably know them well enough to be able to address their concerns and understand their motivations for learning a new skill. Perhaps learning about online technologies at work will help them use similar tools in their personal lives, to communicate more effectively with family and friends overseas. Perhaps they enjoy learning for learning's sake, and it has become part of their personal development plan for the year. Or perhaps you have decided that this is a compulsory skill to have and that you will make it difficult to work in the "old" way. This approach—which takes a degree of courage to pull off, but is strongly recommended—creates a burning platform whereby the team has no option but to jump forward, as there is no way back.

You should also consider the location of your team. Do you all sit together in the same office and have lunch together each day? If that does sound like your team, what benefits would you gain from adding collaboration tools to your project structure? Think about what you need in a project environment: a knowledge repository, a way to share daily project updates, more effective asynchronous and synchronous communication. A colocated team is likely to have methods to address all of these needs—they will just be different methods to dispersed teams who could benefit more from web-based tools.

Don't discount collaboration tools simply because you all work in the same office. Even colocated teams need a knowledge repository, and a project wiki could be hugely beneficial. But you might not need a full-blown enterprise collaboration suite.

Finally, consider the appetite of the team to try something new. It is a lot easier to work with people who are enthusiastic. Consult with your team, share the strategy, and ask for their input around selecting a system. This will help build some enthusiasm and help you avoid jumping in with both feet, only to find that your team members are not behind you.

Using Social Technographics for Profiling

It would be unrealistic to think that all your team would have the same level of enthusiasm for new tools. In 2007, Josh Bernoff and Charlene Li came up with a model to categorize social computing behaviors, and it is still useful today. The main use of the model is to group consumers by the ways they use social media tools to help companies understand how best to manage their social media marketing strategies. This is great if you want to know how to get certain segments of your customer base to interact with you on your corporate website, but the model also has uses for companies planning the deployment of collaboration tools, as it helps you understand the profile of your team and, therefore, contributes to understanding the likely success of any system deployment.

Bernoff and Li call their model Social Technographics, and they updated it in 2010 to include a new rung on the ladder: Conversationalists, as you can see in Figure 7.3. (Bernoff et al., 2010). This reflected, at the time, the increase in the use of Twitter and Facebook for sharing social interactions—"chatting" with their friends. In other words, Conversationalists are people who use social media to stay in touch.

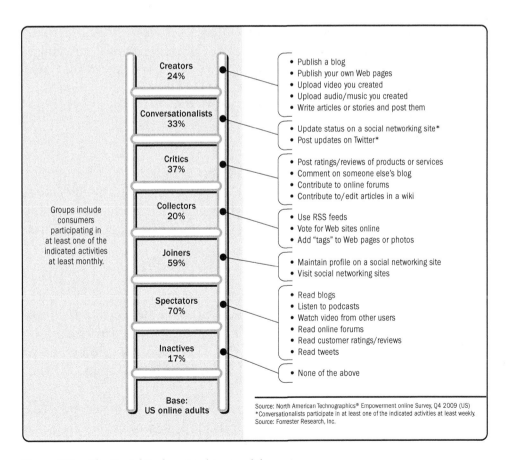

Figure 7.3:   The Social Technographics model.

The authors freely acknowledge that people will fall into multiple rungs on the ladder. Being at the top doesn't automatically mean that you participate in all the behaviors on the lower rungs. The Creators at the top of the ladder (like you and your project team aspire to be) might not be active on social networking sites like Joiners are. Conversationalists might not scour the wider web for their favorite sites on a regular basis. Some people will fall into more than one rung as they participate in multiple behaviors.

Marketers use the Social Technographics model to profile their customer base and establish what social computing tools to use with them. You can do the same for your project team. Ask a few questions of the team at the beginning of the project to work out where they fit on the Social Technographics ladder. It's not an exact science, but knowing the team's background will help shape the way in which you deploy any collaboration technology, or inform which features to focus on first. If you find out that your entire project team are Inactives, you might want to reconsider trialing a collaboration tool with this group of people. Conversely, if all your team are Creators, Conversationalists, and Critics, you will have a very good chance of making your new technology work well.

> You can deploy collaboration tools in an environment where no one has skills and experience in social media or online communication. Make sure that you factor in enough general education, training, and bedding in time to enable the project team to come onboard at their own pace.

Regardless of the Social Technographics profile and other preferences of your team, don't forget that launching a new piece of technology will change the way in which they work. People fundamentally don't like change, which is one of the challenges of project management. Normally, it is the project teams "doing" change to other groups.

Consider the business change principles you adopt when taking a project through from start to finish, and adopt a similar approach for this work. Just because they are your project team, doesn't mean that they will react to change any differently than any other stakeholder group going through a change of working practices.

Project Culture: How are You Going to Pilot Your Software?

You have two choices for how to implement a collaboration tool:

1. Set it up as a project in its own right with a team to manage the deployment and rollout.
2. Deploy it as a tool on an existing or soon-to-start project, and make setting it up part of the project initiation activity.

Whichever you choose (and we'll look more at how you get your tool up and running in Chapter 9), some project has to be the first to use it. Before you start planning your deployment, it is worth giving some thought to what this might be.

Not all projects are equally suitable for proving the usefulness of collaboration tools. Pick a project where your chances of success are higher, and run a trial before rolling out the social media approach to all projects. Ask yourself:

- How long is the project?
- What is the criticality of the project to the business?
- What are the project objectives?

The Timescales

Teams working together on projects of short duration may find that collaboration tools are not as useful as they expected. Projects with a duration of three months or less will rarely generate enough project artifacts to warrant a project wiki. Equally, by the time you have got everyone up and running, the project will be in the closure phase.

Having said that, short projects often don't involve full-time teams and that can be where some of the real benefits of collaboration technology come in—keeping everyone on the same page while you all try to juggle other roles.

Very long projects may be unsuitable for the first-ever project to use a collaboration tool in your organization. It could easily take too long before you are able to report on the success of the initiative. While longer projects are ideally suited to online knowledge repositories, they are not good subjects for a trial, as the PMO will have to wait until the project is closing before evaluating the success of the collaboration system. You could set up interim evaluations to deal with this if you wanted to go ahead and use them on a long project from the outset.

The ideal project length for trying a new tool is three to six months. If you have to test your collaboration tools on a project that will last longer than this, agree on some milestones for evaluating the success of the trial at intermediate points in the project.

The Criticality

All projects add business value, but you would do well to avoid piloting a new way of working with a business-critical project. Anything that is mandatory (for example, making changes to comply with new legislation) does not make for a good trial project. Mandatory and business-critical projects have significant management focus—and the focus is on the deliverables, not on the delivery mechanism. You may find that the adoption of collaboration tools as a trial on this type of project is not welcome, as senior management will see this as a distraction from meeting the business needs of getting the project done as quickly as possible.

Pick a project that has less pressure or lower management attention for your pilot. If that is not possible, at least try to pick a project with a sympathetic sponsor who will support the use of new ways of working together. A sponsor who is prepared for some of the team's time to be taken up with building up the effective use of these tools in the early days of the project will (hopefully) reap the benefits later on when the team increases its efficiency and becomes a tightly knit, delivery-focused group.

Avoid choosing a project that is highly commercially sensitive. Top secret projects should be kept under wraps, and you should not publish data feeds to anyone who wishes to subscribe. Until you've come to grips with how your new system works, including the security privileges, steer clear of using it for anything sensitive.

The Objectives

Finally, consider what the project is going to achieve. Web development projects make excellent projects to trial online project tools—the team is already thinking in a "web" way due to the project deliverables. Look for projects where there is synergy between the project's goals and the methods used to achieve them.

Organization Culture: What Else is Your Company Doing?

While you are busy considering the benefits of adopting new technology in the project environment, elsewhere in your organization there might be other teams already using the tools you would like to use. It is always easier to start from an established base instead of pioneering a path, so it is in your interest to do some investigation into what your colleagues are up to—and it is highly unlikely that your company is doing nothing. Find out who else is using collaboration tools. Who has tried and failed?

Consider:

- What is the appetite for online and collaborative working in the organization?
- What is the current level of activity in the social media space in the organization?

Appetite

Simply through working in your company, you will have a feel for the appetite for the adoption of new things. Is your organization typically trailblazing or does it lag behind with a generally cautious outlook?

Judge the appetite for the use of social media tools. Ask around to see if the marketing and sales teams are doing anything in this space and watch the response: Are they interested and aware of what you are talking about or not at all sure if that is for them?

As you would expect, companies with a greater appetite for new things are more likely to support a project-based social media initiative. However, a lot depends on the PMO and the management of the project management function. Just because the organization generally takes a conservative view to new technology, it does not mean that the idea will get rejected by your direct management team.

Current Activity

Ask around to find out what collaboration tools are in use across the rest of the business, perhaps in overseas divisions if there is nothing closer to home. Learn from what they are doing and if it is something that you can join in with—and want to join in with—then you'll save a lot of the learning curve.

Finally, try to find out if there have been any unsuccessful experiments with collaboration tools. This will help you in two ways. First, it will warn you that the appetite for new technology in your company could be pretty low. Second, it will point out some useful things to avoid when you launch your pilot.

Personal Culture: How Much Time Do You Have to Dedicate to Making this Work?

As the project manager, you will be the key player in making your collaboration system work. You will be instrumental in choosing a platform, implementing it, helping your team use it, and then monitoring their use of it to ensure it really is helping deliver the project more effectively—and it isn't just getting in the way. Think about:

- How much time will you be able to spend learning the tool and then teaching it to the rest of your team and coaching them on it throughout the life cycle of the project?
- How committed are you to making this work?

Managing the Time Required

Different enterprise collaboration tools have different learning curves, and how quickly you will pick up the tool depends on many factors, including your personal technical literacy and, of course, the system itself. Try to talk to some people who already use the tool you are thinking about and ask them how long it took to get up to speed.

Changing the way things are done in any respect normally slows people down. It takes a while to get used to new functionality and the user interface of computerized project management software. Think about the length of time it took you to get comfortable to use scheduling tools. Some companies run three-day courses on the use of Microsoft Project, and while online tools (and project management software in general) are designed today to be far more intuitive, don't underestimate the length of time it will take to become fully conversant in the new technology to the point where using it is second nature.

Getting to that point requires a change in mindset. Being comfortable using the software is not enough—you also need to adopt a mentality that makes it the first place you go for certain activities. It does require a fundamental shift in thinking away from the old ways of doing things and toward the new ways. As with anything, this can take time, but the rewards of sticking with it are well worth it.

The learning curve for a project manager is two-fold, because unless you have a very technically savvy PMO, it is likely that you will be training other members of your team on how to use the tool to the best advantage. So not only are you going to have to learn how to use it yourself, you are also going to have learn how to teach it.

Many tools have online help files, but they don't come with the same kind of user documentation, crib sheets, or manuals that off-the-shelf software has. You might have to write your own how-to guides, personalized to your project management processes, to provide a reference for your team. Talk to other people in your organization or industry to see if they have anything you can reuse.

You should add training tasks to the project schedule: They require planning and management like any other activity. Training doesn't stop, however, after this task is complete. You'll need to find a way to manage an ongoing coaching overhead.

As the "expert" in the tool, you will be asked questions along the way—and if you don't know the answers, you will impede the progress of the tool's adoption. Good project managers coach their teams in the project management process already, so this overhead should be minimal if you build it into your development plans for the team and your general team management activities.

How much time you will need to dedicate to launching a collaboration tool for your project team is very much going to depend on how much process reengineering you do at the same time. If you choose to revamp your processes and rebuild your workflows around your collaboration software, then you will get much deeper levels of engagement. You will also find that it will take a lot more time and require more change management. That's a trade-off you will have to manage internally.

Your Level of Commitment

Your motivation is an important consideration when you are thinking about how to make collaboration work on your project. If your team isn't collaborating now, giving them technology to do it won't get you better results. There is a cultural issue at play there—something that technology alone cannot fix.

Doing something new requires hard work. It will be an uphill struggle to get your new way of working adopted, bedded in, and appreciated by everyone. You might not even get to the point where everyone appreciates it! Adopting collaboration tools on your project can be a great thing to do, with plenty of benefits—but it is not going to be right for every project manager or every organization.

If you've got this far and have decided that software to help you work as a team isn't going to get you better project results, then it is not too late to back out. It will be far more damaging for your team for you to start an "experiment" and then fail to see it through the pilot period, implement it badly, or just give up.

If the thought of all the potential problems is beginning to put you off, skip ahead to Chapter 11 where we look at some of the cyberspace pitfalls and how to avoid them, so that you can give your initiative the best possible chance of success.

So, are you prepared to put in the effort required to make a social media initiative work on your project? If so, read on!

What's Required for Successful Online Collaboration?

Online collaboration tools are generally found in complex project environments. A complex society is defined as having:

- Open systems—these interconnect and are subject to change and instability.
- A degree of chaos—there are uncertainties that you can't plan for.
- The ability to self-organize—groups emerge based on teamwork and shared goals.
- Interdependence—this makes it hard to predict the future on the basis of past experience.

Ali Jaafari from the University of Sydney, Australia, has developed a model for managing projects in a complex, changing environment. He calls it the Creative-Reflexive Model, and the idea is to blend self-organization and creative flexibility with other project management skills to end up with a style of project management that suits environments where there is a high degree of uncertainty and change. "Creative-reflexive project managers are not necessarily members of a particular professional body," he says, "but those who engage in lifelong learning and continuous professional development, act autonomously, believe in shared values, and follow strong personal ethics."

He suggests that the project manager in a complex environment, such as one working in virtual teams and supported by online tools, should be:

- Empowered
- Autonomous
- Open to change to the point of enjoying it
- Able to move beyond applying processes to take a creative approach to project delivery
- Aware of the environmental and project complexities and able to respond appropriately
- Able to apply complexity-reduction techniques to manage the environment without overly controlling it
- Engaged in lifelong learning
- Strongly aware of and following personal ethics (Jaafari, 2003)

Look at deploying a project management collaboration system as a creative enterprise. Work together with your team in a flexible way to take positive advantage of the inherent complexities.

Communicate, Communicate, Communicate

Any change to the way in which people do their jobs should be communicated effectively. Good communication will mean that people know what is coming and how it will impact them. Sending out an email one morning saying that all task assignments will now be allocated through your collaboration tool and that status updates must now be provided online is not going to win your team over and create an environment where online teamwork will thrive.

Talk to your project team and the PMO as you start to formulate your deployment plan. There might be someone who has a lot of experience outside of work who could help you and act as a departmental champion for the new tool.

Summary

Before starting out with deploying collaboration tools, the project manager should consider:

1. The profile of the team
2. The suitability of the project for a trial run
3. Other social media activities within the organization
4. The commitment required to make this work

Manage the introduction of a new tool as a small project, with adequate attention paid to the communication and business change elements to facilitate the new way of working.

CHAPTER 8

Winning Over Management

Once you've decided that you want to introduce collaboration tools to your project environment, you have to convince everyone else. Your strategy, product evaluations, and change management plans will help do this. However, documentation is only the start.

In parallel to your work on assessing the organization's culture and willingness to adopt new ways of working, you can be busy winning over management. This is the Stakeholder Engagement box of Figure 8.1.

Not all senior managers will embrace the opportunity to adopt new technology to support project teams. In particular, you'll face the "if it isn't broke, don't fix it" attitude. In this chapter, we look at how to identify and overcome the concerns from the executive suite. If your senior management team is evangelistic about collaboration and technology, skip this chapter and jump straight into Chapter 9 about choosing the right tool.

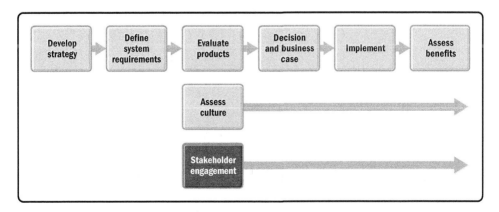

Figure 8.1: From strategy to benefits.

Prepare the Ground

The first thing to consider is how to prepare the way for adopting new technology. Consider this a business change project. You are changing processes and working practices. If you were doing this for a customer, it would be a project with a strong element of business re-engineering and change management.

Carry out stakeholder analysis to identify who needs to know about your desire to adopt new tools, and who will be best placed to support you? You may need to involve:

- The IT department, for technical support
- The HR department, for help with policies around system use for employees
- The Legal department, for guidance on the data management issues of storing information outside of your local geography or firewalls
- The rest of the PMO, for support, assistance, and general championing of the solution
- Your own manager
- Any other senior executives

Once you have identified your stakeholders, you can then canvas their opinions. This group is effectively the senior project stakeholders for your collaboration tool implementation. Try to understand their current position with regard to the use of enterprise tools in the workplace; the results might surprise you.

Senior executives may not be up to speed with current web technologies, so take them through exactly what you are proposing and how these technologies are used by other companies to support their project management activities. Focus on the benefits, like:

- Increased productivity
- Improved team morale
- Better collaboration
- Faster problem solving
- Better efficiencies and reduced rework, and so on

Tie it back to the strategy you prepared in Chapter 6. There should be clear business benefits for wanting to drive through change. Getting them on board early will help them have confidence in the fact that your initiative will be implemented in a clear and measured way, compliant with all relevant corporate policies.

If it helps build confidence and create your case, point out that this initial deployment is a trial. If it doesn't work, there is a route to return to the old ways of doing things.

The deployment of a project collaboration tool is not a corporate communications project. When you talk to senior management about how technology can benefit your team and your project delivery, aim to set the tone for a project that delivers an enterprise collaboration tool, not a communications tool. The risk with a communications initiative is that it will get taken out of the project management environment and merged with the social media initiatives used by marketing or public relations for communicating with customers. While using social media in this way is not a bad thing, the goals of customer outreach and successful project delivery are not closely enough aligned for this to be a sensible approach.

Identifying Risks

Management will probably be concerned about the risks of adopting collaboration tools. As with any project, risk management is key.

Identify risks and present strategies of how to address them as part of your business case.

Some example risks are identified in Table 8.1.

There is also a risk that social media tools are in use without the knowledge of senior management anyway. Only 8% of companies know the scope of shadow IT—that is, technology spending and implementation outside the IT department that includes cloud and online technologies. Over 70% of companies in the same study said they did not know, but wanted to know what was going on outside formal, approved software (Cloud Security Alliance, 2015).

Having a managed deployment of collaboration tools through the PMO with the appropriate involvement of your technical teams will bring this unapproved activity under management control. This is a risk mitigation exercise in its own right.

Tools that support online work-from-anywhere teams can also help offset wider corporate risks. The blizzard that hit the Northeastern United States was estimated to have cost businesses US$500 million

Table 8.1:   Risks associated with launching a project-based social media initiative.

Risk	Mitigation Strategies
Poor take-up means the time and resources invested in the system implementation are wasted and the benefits are not realized.	• Establish a comprehensive implementation method backed up with user training and communications. Monitor take-up on a regular basis and address any failings early.
There is too much information to manage.	• Establish clear guidelines for users, a comprehensive taxonomy of categories and tags, and employ a good search capability. • Adopt a robust housekeeping and archiving strategy.
Stakeholders who are not computer literate miss out on critical discussions and communications.	• Carry out stakeholder mapping to identify which stakeholders are at risk of not receiving communications through the collaboration tool. • Address these gaps using existing methods, or through educating these users and giving them access to the tool.
It will not be possible to tell if the initiative has been a success, as measuring it is too difficult.	• Statistical measures can be employed to demonstrate success. • Anecdotal evidence can also be gathered to demonstrate success. • It may be decided that a formal measurement system is not required.
Employees will spend all day surfing the web and not engaging in business activities.	• Establish a policy that explains what access to these tools can be used for. • Monitor employee activity where it is legally appropriate to do so. • If productivity drops, consider using existing HR processes to address poor performers who are abusing the system.
Our third party partners will not be able to access it. Even if they can, we won't be able to limit what they see and we don't want to share everything with them.	• Provide them with read-only access to the system. • Choose a platform that has permission-based access rights. Set up views in an enterprise collaboration tool so that partners only see what is relevant to them.

by weather analysts, Planalytics (Wagner, 2015). Enabling employees to work more flexibly on their projects and using web-based tools that are accessible from home mitigates against this risk.

Measure Success

Executives like to know that the time and effort spent on launching something new will not be wasted. That is very difficult to promise for any new initiative, let alone one where the benefits are perceived to be intangible, difficult-to-assess things like better team morale. While you can put every effort into deploying your collaboration tool in the best possible way, with full backup and the support of the executive team, the PMO, and everyone else, it is only until you have it operational for a while that you will truly be able to establish whether it has been successful.

In order to measure success, you will have to define what success looks like. Your success criteria may be measures like a 20% reduction in emails relating to the project, or document review and approval within three days instead of the current five. Senior management's success criteria may be different, for example, deployment costs of less than $x and no demonstrable drop in productivity during the change to a different way of working. Find out what is important to management and then work out how to best meet and measure it.

Chapter 6 covers options for measuring the success of your online tools in more detail.

Dispel Myths

What myths and misconceptions exist among your senior managers and what can you do to put them right? You might be surprise about how uneducated your senior management team is about enterprise collaboration tools, especially if they've never used them. However, you are also bound to find some evangelists who have used and loved technology products at other companies and will do what they can to convince you to adopt exactly what they used.

In your project management role, you explain complex concepts to senior stakeholders all the time—so clearing up any misconceptions about what you are trying to achieve should be easy!

Here are some of the common myths around collaboration initiatives and what you can do to dispel them.

Myth #1: It's a Big Change

The first myth to bust is that this has to be a big change. The best approach with launching a new work tool is to start small, so set out the boundaries of your pilot and agree on them with management. Start with the features that will best address the most uncomfortable pain points. As with any other project, having a project charter will enable you to clarify the scope, roles, and responsibilities.

In particular, make sure the administration and system support roles are clearly defined. Are you expecting the IT department to do all of this, or are you taking it on yourself? Agree on the support that you need and ensure that everyone knows how to access it. It's helpful to have your support team involved in the project as early as possible so they fully understand the business goals and how the system is used operationally. This small point addresses the underlying fear that the change will not be controlled.

Myth #2: Anyone Can Do Anything

A strong approach to access controls—no anonymous or generic accounts, for example—will help convince management that there is structure to the technology. It is not a free-for-all, where anyone can write anything.

Finally (at the risk of sounding like a stuck record), have a usage policy. Management will feel more comfortable knowing that employees have received guidance on the use of the system. Training, both in how the tool works and also how they are expected to act while using it, will go some way in alleviating the fear that everyone will be messaging their friends all day. Include a Q&A session where project teams and other stakeholders can ask questions about the use of the tools, the points of policy, company rules, and so on.

Myth #3: Wikis are Problematic

Here are some misconceptions about wikis.

- Wikis are not suitable for a secure environment
- Wikis are anarchic
- Wikis are liable to be hacked
- Wikis don't have sensible access controls
- Wikis will be vandalized by disgruntled employees

All of those things may well be true of public wikis that are not managed effectively, but they certainly are not true of wikis hosted in-house, securely nestled in the firewall. Enterprise wiki software has the ability to set permissions at a granular level, so that access can be controlled appropriately. They can even be linked to the corporate authentication system, so your team can log in seamlessly via single sign-on technology.

Myth #4: No More Face-To-Face Meetings

Another prevalent myth is that the introduction of collaboration tools will negate the need for face-to-face meetings. Colocated working is key for interaction, and the role that body language and tone of voice play in communication is very important. There are many benefits to face-to-face interactions.

Collaboration tools help foster good communication practices and project efficiencies, especially in virtual teams where colocation is not an option. But they will never totally replace the benefits of meeting your colleagues in person, especially when it comes to building workplace relationships.

Myth #5: It Will Waste Time

One of the main concerns that management will raise is that being online is wasting time. If you are not huddled over a spreadsheet, knee-deep in emails, or creating a Gantt chart from sticky notes, then you can't possibly be working. Unfortunately, this is an old-fashioned, but pervasive response to the request to move to more modern, collaborative ways of getting things done.

It is often bosses who feel out of touch or disengaged from what is going on in the team who feel the most concerned about employees wasting time online. It's a way of controlling what gets done and keeping visibility. If this is the concern of your management, explain that, in fact, they will get more visibility of the project activities. You can give them access to the tool and they can follow the discussions and progress in real time. Whether or not they will take you up on this is another matter.

It's not surprising that managers feel that having access to social media sites can result in a loss of productivity when commentators frequently provide examples like the 2013 Ipsos study that concludes individuals spend 3.6 hours on social networks per day.[1]

That's a lot of time. However, there are two factors to take into account with data like this.

First, it's normally a few years old. Studies with results like these abounded three or four years ago. Today, a web search is more likely to turn up surveys like the one from Pew Research Centre that says just 7% of working adults feel their productivity has dropped as a result of Internet, email, and smartphones (Purcell & Rainie, 2014). Research from Deloitte points out that a third of employees have asked for better

---

[1] For more on this survey, see Ipsos. (2013, January 8). *Socialogue: The most common butterfly on earth is the social butterfly*. Retrieved 31 August 2015 from http://ipsos-na.com/news-polls/pressrelease.aspx?id=5954

tools to do their job, but only a third of those received a positive response (Deloitte, 2013). The same study concluded that European workers are up to 20% more satisfied with their workplace culture when they have access to enterprise productivity and collaboration tools, which has implications for employee retention and engagement.

For every negative survey, you can find research supporting the productivity boost that comes from collaborative online working.

Second, before social networking tools were widely available, employees had other ways to waste time, like standing around the water cooler. Think of short bursts of activity on social networking sites as an opportunity for employees to recharge their batteries.

People are often skeptical of surveys and statistics (with good reason), but if nothing else, they show that other companies are making use of these techniques and finding them valuable.

Myth #6: We Can Monitor Individual Activity

This isn't really a myth, as you could take the opportunity to introduce monitoring of employee activities if you can do so and comply with the law. You could, but I don't believe you should, which is why I've included it as a myth.

Undercover monitoring of system usage is legal in some countries, but not everywhere. I would strongly resist all attempts to let management carry out undercover monitoring of what employees are doing on the system or looking at online. Even in situations where your team has behaved impeccably and have never accessed anything they shouldn't, have not spoken out of turn, and have not used any inflammatory or unprofessional language online, monitoring can undermine the product and the concept of online collaboration. Undercover monitoring illustrates that management is not confident in the use (or users) of the tool and this will have an impact on the morale of the project team and their own confidence in the system.

You might not be aware yourself that monitoring is taking place. During the project initiation phase, have a discussion with them about the fact that all electronic communications could be monitored without their knowledge and explain that this is just part of the IT security measures (if this is legal where you are). If it then happens, the team will at least have had some awareness of the possibility and it will hopefully be less of a surprise.

Dealing with Lack of Support

It would be great to think that all project executives and senior managers want is for the project team to deliver excellent projects that contribute business value, regardless of how they go about doing it. But project sponsors and management do take an interest in how you get to the end goal.

Collaboration tools do not sit well with everyone because they are new, and that means they are not perfectly tried and tested, unlike the trusty Gantt chart (and, let's face it, not all project sponsors have managed to learn how to use that yet).

Not all your senior stakeholders will feel comfortable throwing out the old ways and moving to an online world where they have never worked before, especially a marketplace that is so volatile and with so many players. At some point, someone could well be challenging your approach to project management and forcing you to shift your approach back to the old ways, or to ditch the product you have researched and implemented and switch to another one.

The best way to handle management wanting to pull the rug from under your feet is to not let it get that far in the first place. Be prepared to step in to sort out issues and to re-engage your management stakeholders. Identify risks and do what you can to address concerns before they start to have an impact on the reputation of the project and the individuals working on it. Continual stakeholder engagement and sharing the small successes along the way will help address concerns and lack of support among the executive population.

It is in everyone's interest that you and your company stay up-to-date with new technologies and learn to embrace them in a positive and effective way. If you take a bigger picture view, the impact of failure is quite small. Export the project data and try again with another tool.

There is a chance that you might never get that far. Having the discussions about policies and risks might be enough to put some executives off the idea of deploying collaboration tools at all. If all else fails and you cannot convince management to adopt or invest in new technology, should you circumnavigate the bureaucracy and do it anyway? Definitely not. It will undermine your credibility in the workplace and have a detrimental effect on the project team once your little, off-the-record experiment is discovered (and it will be). Wait a while, until you have a more tech savvy project sponsor and try again.

Summary

While many managers are embracing the benefits that social media tools can bring to their businesses, not everyone is as clued into what a collaborative project environment could look like. Manage your stakeholder engagement by:

- Spending some time with executives preparing the ground prior to deploying new tools
- Educating them in the ways that enterprise collaboration tools are used to support productivity in the workplace
- Addressing some of the myths that may prevail in your organization
- Identifying the potential risks that come with adopting new ways of working
- Demonstrating robust risk mitigation strategies to build confidence in the processes and technology
- Showing that you can measure success in whatever form it takes

If management is less than supportive of your initiative and you suspect some unrest among certain members of the executive team, try to address these as soon as possible. The risk of leaving it go too long is that there could be damage to the reputation of the project, the project team, and yourself.

CHAPTER 9

How to Choose and Use the Right Tools

You have a strategy. You know what you are looking for in a tool. You've assessed the change management required and you have a plan for that. You know that you have senior management support.

Everything is in place for you to make the final decision about your tool and get it implemented. This chapter covers the last three boxes of Figure 9.1, moving you from the groundwork through to deployment and evaluation.

First . . . Decide

All the information you have gathered to date gives you everything you need to assess the marketplace and choose a suitable product. In fact, by the time you have gotten this far, you probably already have a strong

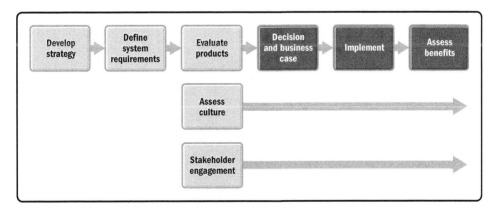

Figure 9.1: From strategy to benefits.

idea of what system you want to use. If not, there's nothing stopping you from making that decision any longer. Demo some systems, use the criteria you developed in Chapter 6 to assess and rank the products, and then decide.

Chosen? Great. Now, let's get a budget approved for your collaboration tool.

Developing a Business Case

The normal approach is to define your strategy, research what you need to do in order to achieve that (both in terms of cultural and nontechnical changes and software/infrastructure investment), and then prepare a business case to secure the investment. When the business case has been approved, you then go into more detail and fully scope the projects or programs required to deliver on that investment.

However, a full financial business case doesn't always stack up for collaboration tools for many reasons, including:

- The difficulties of measuring intangible results like "better collaboration"
- The time it takes to baseline today's results to compare future performance
- It's hard to define exactly what return on investment would look like
- The lack of detailed time recording to see whether improvements have been made in productivity and speed of access to experts

In short, the intangibility and unpredictability of knowledge work makes it hard to quantify anything reliably. Project work by its nature is nonrepetitive, and if you have deployed your collaboration tool at the beginning of a project, you may not have sufficient experience with that team and on that project to estimate, for example, the length of time tasks are taking with any degree of accuracy. Without that baseline, you cannot definitely say that your software has improved the delivery time for tasks. For that reason, many organizations choose not to measure efficiency in a quantitative manner. Instead, companies often rely on employee surveys that, in turn, rely on subjective responses about whether a tool has made it easier to work together. Make an educated guess based on anecdotal evidence and feedback from the project team.

To give another example, it is difficult to quantitatively measure the positive impact of enabling online communications. How much more useful are project work spaces than a phone call? Bloggers in the public online space often use the amount of comments and social shares received on a blog post as a measure of popularity, interest, engagement with their readers, and so on. This is not a reliable measure in a workplace setting: A discussion post may have a couple of comments before you step in and facilitate a face-to-face meeting on the topic, or the commentators make phone calls to get to the bottom of the finer points. The amount of conversation going on is not necessarily a reflection on the quality of those conversations, so again, this is a difficult thing to measure.

The inability to clearly define and measure what you want to achieve will make many project managers uncomfortable (and may force them to choose irrelevant or subjective measures for success). After all, the project charter should include enough detail about scope and acceptance criteria to ensure that the relevant people can sign off the project's products as complete and fit for purpose. You wouldn't embark on a project without knowing what "finished" looks like, and knowing who would agree that the work has been completed to the required quality.

However, do you measure how well you wrote the project charter or how effective your quality reviews were? Probably not, outside a general feeling that it was a good, comprehensive document or that the meeting participants got what they needed from the review. Collaboration tools are a project support system—much like email or conference calls—and would you measure the success of those on a monthly basis? Success criteria are useful, but they do not have to be statistically measurable. Consider the implementation of digital team tools as another option for your project management tool kit. You can measure it with the same judgment calls that you do for the other processes in your methodology.

Don't struggle with a full financial business case unless you really need one to get your investment approved.

The Alternative to a Financial Business Case

If a full financial business case won't stack up, or your leadership doesn't require one, then prepare a short options appraisal instead. Review the solutions available to you using any identified in your strategy document and any others that have come about as part of your general research into delivering the strategy. An options appraisal includes:

- Pros and cons for each option
- Financial investment for each option
- Timescales for implementing each option
- Resource implications for each option
- A recommendation, stating which option you want to go for

Present this to your decision makers and start the discussion to secure the investment in your collaboration tool.

Alternatively, consider asking for approval at this point only for the analysis phase or a small pilot. This would give you a mandate to go ahead and research the market and how the tools might benefit your teams, while not asking for a financial commitment at this point.

First Steps for Implementation

A good way to secure both the investment and the resources required to implement your chosen tool is to start small. Regardless of which product you choose, you still have options. There will be a difference in cost and effort depending on whether your implementation approach is to deploy to one team or to everyone from Day 1.

Also consider starting with the modules that you expect will give the biggest business benefit and add in more features later. Even if the product comes with all the features, you don't have to train your team in how to use them until they are comfortable with the basics (or priority) features. Small and incremental is generally better than big bang for most projects, not just the implementation of collaboration tools.

Planning Your Pilot

This section is a short, generic guide to implementing your chosen product. It assumes that you have already chosen which tool you want to try—if you haven't worked that out yet, go back to Chapter 6 and work through that. It also assumes that you have discussed and answered the questions raised in the previous chapter about change readiness, and that you and your team are ready to go.

Treat It Like a Project

Think about software project management for a moment. Software project managers know all about deploying new systems. They factor in enough time for gathering user requirements, building and configuring the software, and then carrying out robust testing. Bugs are identified and corrected. Software is piloted with small, friendly groups, and the pilot process also includes testing the training course. At the end of a successful software implementation, the users have a tool that will do exactly what they need and they understand how their way of working has changed because of it.

Deploying a collaboration tool is no different to running a software project—or any type of project for that matter. Treat the implementation of your new team tool as a project.

Another facet of a software project is using business change techniques to encourage users to adopt the new system. Humans fundamentally don't like change, and we err on the side of what we know. Ensure that your deployment plan includes sufficient change management activities so that your team of test subjects has the time and motivation to change their behaviors and move toward a culture of working in an online, collaborative way.

Plan and Schedule

Take your task list and create a plan for the work. We're going to assume that you don't need much help to plan the setup and implementation of your project collaboration tool, given that, as a project manager, you plan and implement new things for other people as your job.

Your plan should include a pilot period, a review of the pilot, and some idea of how the software will be deployed more widely if your pilot is successful. Don't forget to also include a period of testing prior to the launch of the pilot to give yourself the best possible start. Web tools typically don't need much testing in a cloud environment, but you will still benefit from giving the product the once-over when it is set up just to make sure that it looks and behaves as you expect.

Finally, your launch plans need to consider what happens to all the project documentation, history, and other artifacts created before the launch of your tool. It is unlikely that you will be able to successfully migrate all that information into the new system. And frankly, you shouldn't attempt it. Information created before the adoption of your online collaboration environment is unlikely to sit well within it. Who wants to type all those project decisions into your collaboration tool just so it has the full project history?

If you have chosen a tool that supports document sharing, then uploading key documents is possible. But forget about migrating everything else. For that reason, it is often easier to start using collaboration tools with a brand new project. It is possible to launch a project-based collaboration initiative midway through a project, but it does involve deciding on how you will manage project information created before your initiative went live.

Review Configuration Options

Each tool is different, but most will allow some form of personalization. The time it takes to do this needs to be built into your plan.

The configuration required for online sites is very easy, and requires no web programming skills. A few clicks and you can be up and running.

Common types of configuration include:

- Adding a logo. Most tools will allow you to add your company or project logo to clearly identify the work space as your own. Some richly featured collaboration tools have free versions that will not offer this functionality. If you upgrade to a paid-for version, you will have more customization options.
- Choosing a color scheme. This is often called a "theme." Some tools will allow you to personalize this completely by choosing your corporate colors, for example. Others will offer you a library of color schemes and let you choose your favorite. Try out a couple: Dark text on a light background looks best. Choose something with strong, contrasting colors, and ask any color-blind members of your team to check that they can read everything clearly.
- Setting up alerts and reminders. How do you want to find out that something has changed? Consider setting up alerts or email reminders for the whole team, although you might not want to do this from Day 1 while you are still adding test content. Project stakeholders, the steering group, and the sponsor might want to receive alerts only about issues of concern to them, so check out the tailoring options to make sure that you don't bombard these stakeholders with lots of irrelevant information.

- Creating user profiles. Each user will have a user profile that displays information about them. Use real names: No pseudonyms or users simply called "admin." Add photos if possible, along with contact information.

- Setting permissions. You don't want all your users to have administration rights, as they could accidentally delete all kinds of relevant project data. (As an aside, check what recovery options are available for data deleted by accident.) Some tools offer levels of site permissions, so set up your users with the correct profiles. You will probably want full administration rights, but choose someone else to share that responsibility with you. That way the other administrator can still make updates and changes, fix problems, or restore deleted documents if you are on holiday or off sick for any length of time.

- Choosing a default language. If your software is going to be used by a global team, think about what language the interface will display in. It might be possible to customize the user profiles so that team members who wish to access the site in their native language can do so. Don't force team members to use English where it is not necessary. Note that this is different than choosing a language for communication between international team members. Even if the user interface displays in their national language, you may want to mandate that the language the team communicates in is something different.

- Choosing time zones. Where are your team members based? If they are not all in the same time zone, then consider how times will display on the site. If a team member in Germany posts a discussion topic, will it display the time where she is, or the time where the administrator is? If you can only set one time zone, choose the time zone where most of the team is based. It is better to set time zones per user, specific to the location of that user. Make sure that everyone understands this has been done, so that there is no confusion. You don't want your Mexican developer making a phone call at 3 p.m. to the Indian project manager, because he thought she had just updated the project work space—when really she made the update at 2:30 p.m. her time, and has now left the office.

- Setting up and downloading apps. If the collaboration tool you are using comes with an app, get it on your tablet or phone and check that your configured interface looks okay.

Configuring the site to look exactly how you want it does not need to take long and gives a professional finish. The systems are designed to get you up and running in a very short amount of time, so having a committee or a work-stream team dedicated to doing this will be overkill. You will spend longer creating the work-stream terms of reference than you will in setting up the tool.

A better approach is to configure it yourself (or ask a nominated individual to do so) and then let the team take a look. Ask some of them to test it out and give you feedback. When it is used in earnest, it will be clearer to see what could be done differently, or better. Build these suggestions in as continuous improvements.

Watch Out for Customization

"Customization" means something very different from "configuration." It involves changes at the level of the software code to create functionality bespoke for your company, for example, a particular workflow. Customization creates issues when new versions are released: There are no guarantees that your customized workflow, for example, will still function when the rest of the application is upgraded to the latest version. Avoid systems that expect you to customize unless you have a dedicated software team and a large budget.

Going Live

The tool is chosen, configured, and tested. You have run a successful pilot. You are now ready to officially launch it to a wider group.

By this point, your team will know that the new tool is coming, and have already seen the test version. They might even have been involved with the pilot, or spoken to people who have, so there should be a good buzz about the launch of the new tool.

There are two options for the launch of a collaboration tool—a big bang approach or an organic approach.

In a big bang approach, a particular date is chosen and that is the day that the tool is "switched on." This can be accompanied by posters, balloons, a lunch-and-learn session, or whatever else your company normally does to celebrate a new project going live. If you prefer to keep the launch quiet, then do so. This is often preferable if the new system is only going to be used by a small subset of people who would see those posters. Either way, the tool becomes operational on that specific date and all team members are expected to use it.

The alternative, organic approach is to let the trial period drift into operational usage. Once you are comfortable that the trial has been a success and that you want to launch the tool to a wider audience, set up logins and passwords for other team members and let them explore and adopt it at their own pace.

While this sounds like a risky strategy—what happens if no one uses it?—bottom-up adoption is the way social media tools spread online and in organizations. There is a very good chance that this will be a successful way to grow the usage of your application with very little effort. This is also called "viral" adoption, referring to how quickly viruses can spread.

Keep an eye of the utilization of the tool and if it is not as you expect, or if you notice that one team member in particular is dragging behind and not using it, you can consider mandating the use of the tool for particular tasks from a particular date, or putting in place other lower key strategies to encourage the new way of working. Getting everyone to complete their user profile can be an easy way to encourage new users to try out the tool.

If you have opted to introduce functionality over time, make it clear at the time of launch just what functionality is "switched on." If there is a placeholder for a wiki, try to hide the link so that people don't click it and then find out there is nothing there. Or add a short descriptive text along the lines of "coming soon." Consider this Phase 1 of the launch of your system. There is always time to add in more features later, but you will never have enough time to undo the damage done by a poor implementation.

Recruit a Champion

You will obviously be championing for a wide take-up of your online collaboration tools, but think about who else you could recruit as a champion for the cause. One or two key project users could make a huge difference to both selling the benefits and encouraging other users to adopt the new technology. Champions don't have to be the most senior person in the team, or the person seconded to the project from the IT department. Look for a champion who is:

- enthusiastic about new technology and social media, even if they have little practical experience;
- may already be online and using social media tools in their personal life;

- well-connected within the project team and who will end up working with everyone else, or at least a large cross-section of the project team; and
- good with people and able to help out coaching other team members.

Go-Live Checklist

✓ User accounts are set up

✓ Reminders and alerts are configured for each team member

✓ Training has been carried out and user guides are available as a memory jogger for anyone who needs them

✓ The project team knows where to access the social media tool and whether it is available from mobile devices

✓ The project team knows what policies apply to the use of the tool

✓ The project team understands what the tool is going to be used for and how to access project artifacts created before the tool was launched

✓ The project manager understands who will *not* be using the tool, and has a strategy in place to ensure these stakeholders still get the information they need

Making it Easy to Use

"Can you send me the link to that website again?" This is not something that you want to hear in every team meeting. With all the online data, company websites, intranets, extranets, document management systems, and so on that any organization has, your collaboration tool is at risk of getting lost.

The type of tool that you deploy will have an impact on where it is stored or accessed from. Essentially, make it as easy as possible for project team members to find the tool, as this will encourage them to use it.

Here are some tips for helping team members find your collaboration tool online:

1. If you use a shared network drive for document storage, create a short text file or document with a list of the relevant links and store it somewhere easy to find. This will act as a memory jogger for people who have forgotten the link.

2. Create an easy-to-remember URL. http://www.social123-tools.mycompany/project-x/201_03654default.aspx?login is not easy to remember. A link like http://www.projectX/blog is easy to remember. Talk to your IT department about setting up a redirect on the link to your collaboration site. All this means is that you type in the shorter, easier URL and you are automatically routed to the longer, more complicated one that you can never remember.

3. Try to fit your new tools into your existing project management information system framework. For example, if you use software like Microsoft SharePoint, include a section of favorite links with a direct link to the collaboration tool landing page.

4. Add the relevant links to your team's browser favorites. Your IT support team may be able to do this remotely. It is very easy to do. From the social media page, go to the Favorites menu in Internet Explorer, then select "Add to Favorites." In Mozilla's Firefox browser, the menu is called Bookmarks. From this menu, select "Bookmark this page." Other browsers have the same functionality although it may be called something different again.

5. If you have more than one collaboration tool available to your team, consider creating a landing page for your project. This will be the first place to go for all the links and means that you don't have to remember multiple URLs.

6. Talk to your PMO. What systems do they already have in place that form part of the existing tool set or the project management processes for your company? There might be something there that can be adapted or added to for your collaboration app. Avoid reinventing the wheel if at all possible. If your team is used to going to the PMO intranet site, capitalize on that and simply add another link from there to your collaboration tool.

7. Ask your IT team to make it so that the collaboration tool link opens automatically when you switch on your computer in the morning.

8. Download the app version to tablets and mobiles.

9. The easiest way to drive adoption and make it easy to use is to make the browser home page point to your collaboration

tool's main welcome screen. Many companies have policies that state your browser's default home page is an intranet or other corporate site. If you can get around that, set the default to your collaboration tool.

Finding your collaboration tool is one thing—getting into them is another. As all the tools require you to identify yourself, they expect the user to log in with a distinct username and password. If you are anything like me, you already have a hundred and one passwords to remember for various time-tracking systems, email applications, other software, and websites. Each new app that you add to your project management tool kit is another password for your team to remember.

Talk to your IT department about the possibility of using a single sign-on approach. This means having one password—normally the one you log on to your computer with in the morning—which links to all the others behind the scenes and automatically logs you on to all other applications without you having to do anything additional. This can be an enormous time (and sanity) saving option for your project team members, but it is also a relatively complex piece of additional work for your IT team.

An alternative is to ensure that "cookies" are enabled on the computers of your team. A cookie is data stored on your computer by the web browser that remembers certain information, for example, user preferences. If you browse to a website that requires you to log in, and your username is already stored in the correct field, that data has been populated by a cookie.

Cookies can store the usernames and passwords for the websites you use to minimize the need to type them in again. However, this is not recommended for computers that are shared, for example, in a software testing lab or a project war room. Cookies are also used by websites to track user behavior and provide marketing data to companies. For these two reasons, some organizations prevent the use of cookies on office computers, so get some advice from your IT department about what would work most effectively for you.

Evaluating the Benefits

The launch of a new tool can be an exciting time, but don't expect it to revolutionize the way you manage projects overnight. Adoption of anything new takes a while, so although you could start seeing the benefits instantly, it is more likely to be a month or so before the project team really starts realizing the efficiencies of working in this way. Schedule time to review the success of your collaboration tool against the objectives of your strategy and your business case.

However, you may never truly realize the full benefits, as some of your stakeholders may refuse or be unable to get on board despite all the change management and stakeholder management you've done. For example, team members in countries with poor technology links may not find it possible to use the new tool. Replacing your weekly conference call with a webinar may exclude them from team communications completely. This highlights why it is so important to invest time in identifying who can and will use the tool before you get to the point of launch.

The next section will look at how to manage poor take-up, regardless of the reason.

What Happens if Take-Up is Poor?

Even with the best, well-thought through deployment plan, it is possible that some people will not get on board for your collaboration revolution. Adoption of the tool across your project team is essential to making the most of the productivity and engagement benefits. Poor take-up of a new app can be the death knell for your initiative: After all, it is hard to collaborate effectively if some of your team are not connected online.

If adoption is poor, you could mandate the use of your online system for project purposes. However, this is likely to further alienate those users who refuse to come on board. The best approach to gaining wide-scale adoption of your tool is for users to establish for themselves that it is the best way to get things done. If they can see the benefits, they will use the tool. Your deployment plan should include plenty of information about "what's in it for me" and the benefits from using the tool.

Let's assume that despite your best efforts, you still have some people who are not using the tool. What next?

Is There a Culture of Sharing?

What is the psychology of information sharing in your organization? Is there sharing or hoarding? Collaboration initiatives are based on the premise that information should be shared. Unfortunately, some corporate cultures do not reflect this. Knowledge is very rarely power in a corporate environment, although many managers behave as if this is the case. An organizational culture that does not support sharing and fosters knowledge silos is not a good culture for collaboration tools.

Ensure that people do not feel vulnerable by sharing information or participating online. Enterprise collaboration tools in project teams actually have a head start on other internal social media initiatives because the team has to work together to get things done, and you are creating new artifacts, documentation, and knowledge. Start by encouraging people to share this "new" information that particularly relates to the business of the project.

You can slowly turn around this type of culture and you can create a little pocket of project information sharing, even within a larger, non-supportive culture. But it will be an ongoing challenge and the necessary support from senior management may not be in place.

Why Don't People Contribute?

Sotirios Paroutis and Alya Al Saleh from Warwick Business School spent time at a multinational technology and services corporation investigating the reasons why individuals do (or do not) contribute to the online tools in use at that company.

Employees who did contribute to the social media initiatives within the company cited reasons such as effective communication, generating discussion about new ideas, finding solutions to problems, and staying up-to-date with the activities of colleagues. They were also motivated by building their own personal and professional networks, building credibility within the organization, and by helping others.

Most of the employees who were asked why they did not contribute to the tools said they didn't have enough time. They also said that they lacked knowledge of how the tools worked and why they were useful, and they were cynical about the value that social media could provide to the organization. Some believed that management did not support online collaboration and networking initiatives, both in terms of communicating the benefits and in rewarding those who did take part. There was also a feeling that having more information led to conflicting data, reliance on nonreliable sources, and lower accuracy. The status quo was another common reason people gave to explain why they had not adopted new technologies: It is difficult to move from the comfortable ways currently in use (Paroutis & Al Saleh, 2009).

Understanding the reasons why people do not want to participate is the first step in working out how to address this challenge.

Stakeholder Mapping: What are They Missing?

Identifying all the stakeholders and mapping their role on the team to the functions provided by the new tools will give you an idea of what they will miss out on by not taking part in your online collaboration. For example, although your project sponsor may have access to the app on his tablet, he may prefer to receive updates in the old-fashioned way. There will be holdouts and these people cannot be excluded from the project or the team. If it is within your control, you can strongly encourage people to use the new tools with extra training and bring the rest of the team onboard for encouragement and support. But if it is executive stakeholders, then you may have to accept that your influencing skills will not change their minds. If this is the case, don't spend any time building customized views into the project data online.

You can also go back to your Social Technographics profiles and work out if extra support is required for the stakeholders who fall low on the ladder.

Easier Access to the Tool

Make sure everyone can access the collaboration tool as easily as possible. We've looked at some ways to do this earlier in the chapter.

Are There Other Issues in the Team?

Remember, collaboration tools alone will not drastically improve your projects. The use of apps will enable better, more timely communication in a dispersed team and more effective knowledge sharing. They can help you spend less time looking for documents and can make it easier for you to collaborate on paperwork across time zones. But if you are managing a team that fails to work together at the moment, giving them a whole load of technology options won't address those underlying issues. If your team is not working effectively together offline, then chances are they won't work effectively together online either.

"If a dispersed team is not communicating well, it may not be because of the dispersal," say Susan Bloch and Philip Whiteley in their book, *How to Manage in a Flat World* (2009). "Some team members are not on speaking terms with one another even though they are all in the same open-plan office. Their communication, and possibly their relationships, might actually be improved if they were on opposite sides of the world."

Sort out the team issues that are not down to technology. Resolve those ongoing disputes and get rid of the unnecessary conflict. Collaboration tools can help a project team move to being highly performing, but only if the team was actually working beforehand.

Set a Good Example

This should go without saying, but use the tools yourself! Demonstrate your commitment to the new ways of working through your actions.

Make it Fun

Revisit your gamification options. Have a quiz where users have to hunt online for the answers. Give a prize to the longest sustained discussion thread over the course of a week. Run a lunch-and-learn session. Have a train-a-friend challenge, where everyone has to show someone else a feature that is new to them. Change all your profile photos to cartoon characters for a day. Set up a Really Simple Syndication (RSS) feed to pull in the weather, TV listings, the office cafeteria menus—anything that will get the team to look at the tool, and then continue using it.

Make it Useful

If gamification isn't for you, then think about what else you can add to the project work space to encourage people to visit and use it. Include news feeds from the latest academic thinking in the field or from the trade press. Maybe the team members would benefit from links to sites providing educational, mentoring, or development activities? The better you know what motivates your team, the easier it will be to find content that draws them to the tool, above and beyond the uses for managing the project successfully.

Buddy Up

Forget the generation gap: It might not be the older members of your team who have the most difficulty in adapting to new ways of working. Pick the most enthusiastic and technically-literate users and ask them to partner with the reluctant users. It is often easier to sit with someone and talk them through what the tool can do and the benefits this can bring to their working practices. A peer-to-peer conversation and coaching session can be more effective than the project manager running a training session, especially as the person being buddied up will probably feel more comfortable asking "stupid" questions in this environment.

The buddy system does not need to last for the duration of the project; it just needs to last until the reluctant users have gotten a better grasp of the system and are comfortable with using it on their own.

Buddying can also be a useful development exercise for project team members. It gives technically literate team members the opportunity to share their skills in a safe environment, which can be a trial run for taking on a coaching or mentoring role. Also consider pairing up people who would not normally need to work closely together on the project. This will give each partner the opportunity to spend time with someone they wouldn't normally spend time with, and will help cement working relationships in the project team.

Blend Old and New

There is a way around this that avoids mandating the use of a new tool and alienating your team members from the project management process. You have a raft of conventional project management tools. Don't throw them all out to be replaced by one online collaboration product. This risks dividing your user group into the "in-the-knows" and the "ignoreds." All project management relies on great communication and people skills, so blanking a portion of your stakeholder group by dropping conventional communication channels is an approach destined for disaster. Instead, blend the new media and the old conventional tried-and-tested methods to find something that is appropriate for your situation and suitable for your project and team.

Creating a sensible blend of both old and new techniques does come with a catch. Did you spot it? It is more work for the project manager. You will end up supporting and maintaining potentially more ways of communicating with your stakeholder groups. And that is time consuming. However, think of the payoffs.

The main business benefit behind using collaboration tools for project management is to save time in the long run through better communication and effectiveness of delivery. Focus on what you want to achieve through using the tools—old and new—and then choose the most appropriate tool to get the job done. Blending the two approaches together will give you more opportunities and the ability to have a greater impact on project productivity.

However hard you try, you might find that your collaboration tool simply doesn't take off. There is no point flogging a dead horse. You tried it; it didn't work. If you are still passionate about the benefits that collaboration technology can bring to your project (and you should be), then leave it until another project and try again, perhaps with a different product. Next time, though, look at the deployment strategy you used. What can you do differently to overcome the difficulties of getting your social media activity off the ground?

Summary

This chapter covered the business case and implementation planning for getting your collaboration tool set up and running. Additionally, it looked at:

- Configuration over customization
- Making collaboration tools easy to find and use
- Addressing the challenges of adoption within the early weeks of the system use

CHAPTER 10

Getting Started With Collaboration Tools: Using Wikis

Full collaboration solutions can take a while to get set up and get started. Many software providers will tell you that you can create a project in a few clicks, but you still need to input the data for your project and team to get the best out of it. There is configuration effort involved in every solution if you want to use it effectively.

Standalone wikis are not full-scale collaboration tools and they have a very low barrier to entry. They are based on free or cheap software that can be managed behind the corporate firewall so they don't suffer from the same security concerns that management may worry about with online, cloud-hosted solutions. For more on security challenges, see Chapter 12.

For these reasons, and to support project managers wanting a fast, cheap option to get started with collaboration tools, wikis deserve an in-depth look. This chapter looks at wikis and how you can use them within a project environment for a variety of knowledge-sharing activities. Wiki functionality is often incorporated into fully-featured collaboration software as well, and this chapter also serves as a practical guide to those who want to use the in-built wiki tools within their existing tool set.

Wikis Explained

"Wiki" is Hawaiian for "quick." It's also an acronym of "What I Know Is" (Leadbeater, 2009). A wiki is a collection of web pages that are written by a group of people, normally on a particular topic—your project, in this case. The wiki acts as a knowledge repository. Wiki software makes it easy to add pages and link them to other pages, which creates a hyperlinked data set. In essence, a wiki is the collective knowledge from your project team, organized in web page format.

Wikis encourage knowledge dissemination: They provide an easy-to-use format for dumping all that project information out of your team's heads and organizing it in a way that makes it useful for others.

The Advantages of Wikis

Wikis are a powerful tool when set up and used correctly. Here are some of the benefits you could expect to see.

- This type of knowledge repository is useful for long-term projects where staff turnover is high. It is a way of capturing what people know before they leave the team, so wikis can also be used when you have specialists seconded to the project for a short period.
- They discourage knowledge silos. Team members create a collaborative knowledge base, and will see how knowledge areas overlap on the project through the hyperlinked structure of the wiki.
- Wikis are customizable, so you can tag and organize content in a way that makes logical sense to the project's objectives.
- Wiki software tends to come with good search facilities and this makes it better than email folders when it comes to retrieving relevant information.
- They are a good tool at project handover and act as a summary of all the project's knowledge for the operational team.

A further advantage to a wiki, as with other sources of written communication, is that they are often better for cross-cultural teams. The spoken language barrier can sometimes prevent fluent spoken conversations. Those team members without English as their first language are typically much better at writing than they are at expressing themselves during a conversation, when the pressure is on to get the words out and the grammar correct. Written updates allow them the time to express themselves adequately. This won't, of course, be the case for everyone.

Wiki Disadvantages

There are downsides to every tool and the main ones to point out for wikis are:

- A successful wiki has more than one page. While it's quick and easy to get started, it does take time to build a successful wiki.
- Team members need to be guided around what will make a useful wiki entry.
- Team members should understand how to avoid making duplicate entries. Knowledge integrity is key to creating a good knowledge repository. Two entries on the same subject could jeopardize this, especially if they both have slightly different versions of the "truth."
- Wiki software is easy to use and comes with a "what you see is what you get" text editor so there is no coding required. However, team members need to think in a "web" way to provide intelligent links to other entries in the wiki. Flat (non-linked) articles about project topics are useful, but the power in a wiki comes from linking the information to other relevant topics. Not all teams will be set up to think this way, and not all team members will be able to make the creative leap from entering data in the wiki to linking it to other entries.

Review Your Taxonomies

Manage the amount of data generated by a successful project wiki (or any other collaboration tool) by reviewing the information architecture and taxonomies in use. These categorize your content, making it easier to navigate and search. In the early days, you won't have that much content to worry about, but once the software is embedded in the way the team works, then the content will become harder to manage. Good categorization then becomes more important.

Adrian Wible, coauthor of the book, *97 Things Every Project Manager Should Know* (2009), suggests categorizing wiki pages by the type of person who will be using them. For example:

- "**Stakeholders**. Have space for topics such as up-to-the-minute project status, short-term issues, long-term issues, risk, budget tracking, and milestone achievements.

- **Developers**. Add information, such as the connection string to connect to the QA database. Fellow programmers won't waste time trying to locate the code from other random sources. Team members can share information on topics like coding standards, build and deployment procedures, common pitfalls, and use of advanced coding techniques such as dependency injection...
- **Business analyst**. Often this person is not colocated in the developer work space. This is a perfect space to centralize access to working documents and domain artifacts that can be accessed from multiple locations.
- **Testers**. The organizational structure may separate testing responsibility from the programmer. This site can provide a clearinghouse between the two teams. Post topics like how to use testing tools. Bug-tracking procedures can be developed and discussed online, and the final decisions posted here" (Wible, 2009).

You could come up with other ways of structuring your wiki, but make sure that whatever you use makes logical sense to you and the other members of the team and avoids duplication.

Wikis as Organizational Knowledge Repositories

It would be great if all your project team members sat together and shared the lessons they learned each week by having a chat by the coffee machine. In real life, that doesn't happen. People work in different buildings, from home, on the road, or in different countries and time zones. A lot of project management in these situations is done by email, or through discussion threads in a collaboration tool. The trouble with both these systems is that the knowledge often ends up getting lost, deleted, or filed away somewhere where it is difficult to find later. It is also often poorly targeted, with multiple recipients, some of whom are not the slightest bit interested in learning about what was done.

A project wiki can alleviate those difficulties by storing relevant project knowledge in a single space, and target information to those who need it through the subscribe feature.

Wikis are not a replacement for collaboration tools or email, but they can provide a secure and searchable repository for capturing lessons learned and other types of organizational knowledge such as configuration elements for different system deployments.

Wikis in Action: Project Management

A project manager in a healthcare company was tasked with rolling out a new medical software program to over 30 different hospitals. Each hospital deployment was to be broadly the same, but she knew they would each have slightly different requirements. For example, the smaller hospitals would need fewer additional PCs; the larger hospitals would need additional printers. Training requirements would differ depending on the size of the team at each location.

She set up a project wiki based on Microsoft SharePoint. This contained an entry for every hospital. As her small team carried out site visits, they recorded the information about each location in the wiki. All the discrepancies and unique characteristics were noted, and the entries were annotated with more information as they got further through each deployment.

This data repository meant the team had a central location to store information and prevented them from having to either remember or rely on email for those details. The team was made up of five people, and while they may have been able to share the information between themselves during regular team meetings, it was beneficial to have a reference source.

At the end of the multiyear project, the wiki was handed over to the IT service delivery team, which was able to see which hospital had what equipment installed.

Wikis for Lessons Learned

We need to move past the concept of "lessons captured" and really embed and improve lessons learned in project management.[1] A lessons learned database is the tool with the most potential to improve project performance, closely followed by the action of collecting lessons learned itself (Besner & Hobbs, 2013).

Wikis are good for this, as you can capture lessons learned alongside the institutional knowledge that is being created as the project unfolds.

You can create a separate section of your wiki for lessons learned or use a separate wiki as a departmental lessons learned database for all

---

[1] Improving the post-implementation review/lessons learned process is the subject of another of my books, *Customer-Centric Project Management*.

project managers and their teams to contribute to. In this case, the tool needs to be run by someone who can manage it on an ongoing basis to ensure that updates and housekeeping do not stop when one particular project stops.

The NASA Lessons Learned Database

A great example of capturing and sharing lessons learned in a database is the NASA Lessons Learned System (accessible at http://llis.nasa.gov).[2] This publicly accessible database provides access to official, reviewed lessons from NASA projects that have fed into continuous improvement for future initiatives.

There are a number of ways to display the same information: By NASA Center, by Mission Directorate, by topic, or by year. Each of these choices applies filters to help users narrow down the search results. You can search within the filtered results as well.

Each entry has a descriptive title, abstract (so you can quickly see what the content is about without having to click into the detail), full details, the lesson learned and follow-up recommendations, and then the topics that this applies to. Some include images.

Your lessons learned wiki could be set up in a similar way, although probably on a smaller scale!

First Steps With Wikis

Wikis are a great place to dip your toe into the waters of collaboration tools because they offer the authors and the organization a lot of control. They are very structured. Wiki posts can be attributed to a particular author, and a specific date and time of publication. Further updates and additions are linked to their authors so there is a full audit trail of what was changed and when. Wikis offer a very safe and robust environment for trialing a new way of working, which can be beneficial if you sense resistance from either the team or executive management. Chapter 8 discusses more about how to convince senior management that social media tools are a useful addition to your project management arsenal.

---

[2] Accessed 31 August 2015. All data correct at that date.

It is easiest to start a project wiki at the beginning of a new project. Include it as part of the initiation activity. However, you might want to wait until you have some content in there (created by you and the team) before you tell your wider stakeholder group about it. There is no point in them accessing information that is not up-to-date, or worse, finding there is no information there at all. You will very quickly lose the good-will of that community and you will find that they won't come back to hunt for information again.

Choose and Install Your Tools

There are a number of wiki platforms available. You may find that wiki features come with your project collaboration software if you are using one. If not, there are plenty of standalone tools available, all of which have broadly similar features and several of which are free.

Software that you can host on your own internal company network is more appropriate for project wikis, as the wikis will be available to staff only. Make sure that whichever product you use can be hosted internally and is not publicly available: Sometimes you get "free" in exchange for your data being available online with no security.

Think about how people will be accessing the tool. Options are:

- A specific URL they store in their favorites
- A link on your company intranet
- Via an app or on their smartphone
- Through the enterprise project management system or collaboration tools

In practice, the project team will access the wiki from a variety of sources, so think about how you can make it widely accessible as this makes it easy to use.

My recommendation is that you don't let an internal IT developer build you a bespoke solution. Even if you have really talented developers, using something that is tried and tested elsewhere, with a developer community committed to keeping it up-to-date and with regular additions of new features, is preferable. It will be faster to get going and easier to maintain than something written in-house.

If your IT team is interested in what you are doing with the wiki, then get them involved by helping you choose a platform and perhaps doing some customization to get it looking exactly how you would like.

Look and Feel

The "look and feel" of a website refers to how it appears on the screen and what the user interface is like. Project wikis do not need flashy animation and pop-up boxes. They are a workplace tool, and as long as they are intuitive and easy to use, they'll do just fine. Think clean, professional, and functional, not ugly and clunky.

You may prefer a tool that allows you to customize the look and feel, adding, for example, your company logo or color scheme. This can help embed the tool in operational practice and encourage corporate use.

Empower Your Authors

Set up your team members to have access to the wiki and empower them to update it frequently. Any time spent updating the wiki or recording information is time away from completing other project deliverables. But the benefits of a long-term knowledge repository for your project are significant. Task your team with knowledge sharing and fostering team spirit, both of which a wiki can help with.

As project manager, you should expect to be one of the main authors. This is because it's your role to facilitate knowledge sharing and capture and to think about lessons learned. You'll often see something on an email or hear something in a meeting that you feel warrants recording formally, and unless you have a project administrator to help you, then it will fall to you to record those facts.

Review Regularly

A wiki that is not regularly reviewed and "pruned" will fall into disrepair. Like any software tool, it is only as good as the data you put into it. If the data cannot be subsequently retrieved, you'll find people stop updating it and stop using it.

Schedule regular reviews where you skip quickly through the wiki looking for:

- Orphaned pages (those that don't link to anything else)
- Broken links
- Pages that are out-of-date or that haven't been updated for a certain period (this will depend on your project's current phase and overall duration—six months is a good maxim)
- Categories that no longer have relevance

- Pages that are not in any categories
- Images, documents, and other files that have disappeared or been deleted

If your wiki tool comes with standard reports (or if you have a talented IT colleague who can write some), then you can create reports to identify these issues automatically and save yourself a job.

Good housekeeping will keep your wiki maintained, relevant, and useful.

Wikis in Action: Program Management

Senior stakeholders can benefit as much as the project team from the implementation of social media tools. "We primarily use our wiki as a communication tool and central repository for project and operations tracking," says Bonnie Cooper, PMP, an IT Program Director, from Waltham, MA. "At the steering level, I have a page that has one two-column table that states business goals on one side and the technical means to achieve them. Then, we have another four-column table that identifies key projects, status, milestones, and due dates."

Cooper also uses graphics to illustrate progress and pastes a snapshot of the most up-to-date dashboard into the wiki, along with a list of results to date, such as previous launches and other project accomplishments.

"The key for this level of program reporting is to identify the strategy and show all activity in the program related to reaching the business goals," Cooper explains. "The idea is to unite the business silos to be an effective governing body, especially as we try to negotiate for constrained resources. We also have links to other working team pages, like back office systems and website operations, so folks can navigate through the program looking for more details."

The wiki was also valuable during an audit. "As part of our preparation for a system audit, we set up a series of child pages identifying key processes that the system supported," Cooper says. "We used a template that identified the process, key rules, exceptions, what worked, what didn't, and future goals. It turns out that the wiki is becoming a central repository for knowledge around this system." The more the team uses the wiki, the more valuable the data in it becomes, and it now includes links to information and attached documents that further delineate each business process.

Cooper's team uses the wiki in-team meetings, where they display relevant pages and edit them in real time. "I'm not sure that folks are actively looking there outside the meetings, but we are trying to encourage this," she says. "I include the link in email status reports, which we still use and I am also experimenting with the social functions in LiquidPlanner as a way to provide a whole bunch of information about a project, including task details, and I reference that via the wiki site."

Dealing With Revisions

Wikis allow other people to revise your content. They can correct a small spelling error or fundamentally rewrite the whole page to give it a different meaning. Wikis are collaborative knowledge repositories, which means you have to accept that you'll work on the content together.

A concern here is that there is the chance that incorrect data will get added, either in error or maliciously. This is a risk, but if the wiki is well-used, other users will see the error and correct it.

Let the team edit each other's work; it's no different than collaboratively working on a document and having different people making changes. It also promotes an environment of trust.

Subscribe

Consider choosing wiki software that has a feature to allow you to subscribe to updates. This will send you an email each time an article is added, amended, or deleted. It's an easy way of keeping on top of changes without having to go into the wiki every day to hunt for them.

Sign your team up for alerts as well.

Search

The search is probably the most important feature of a wiki, so you should definitely make this one of your software selection criteria. Wikis are organic, and a single entry can spawn many subpages. After a while, especially on complex and long projects, the wiki navigation will have evolved to work best with search.

Tagging entries with keywords and adding categories will give you better quality search results. You should also ensure each piece has a

Table 10.1:   Sample categories for wiki pages.

Suitable Categories for Wiki Pages	
Risks	Configuration
Issues	Budget
Quality	Contracts
Plans	Estimating
Announcements/Communication	Team management
Scope	Dependencies
Lessons learned	Other projects
Requirements	Handover to operations
Change control	Project-specific content

"date last updated" date. Then you can select these older pieces for update to ensure the integrity of the wiki stays high and that the content remains relevant.

When you first set your blog up, give some thought to how people will be searching for information in three months' time. You can always add new categories later, but it helps to have as comprehensive a view as possible at the outset. Examples of suitable categories for wiki pages are given in Table 10.1.

Wiki Mistakes

As with any new tool, it's easy to make mistakes when you are starting out. Your wiki may only be aimed at a small project team, but if you get off to the wrong start, you may have damaged the implementation before you have really had a chance to start. Here are some things to avoid.

Anonymity: The Big No-No

However tempted you are to allow people to post to the wiki or edit pages anonymously, don't do it. People must use their real names when they publish wiki content. It forces them to give more thought to their writing. It is very easy to be disparaging (or downright rude) when no one knows it is you. This is a professional forum for project communication, so ensure everyone is encouraged to act that way.

Perfection: Don't Bother

Use a built-in spellchecker if your wiki tool has one. However, don't worry too much about spelling and grammar, as long as the point is clear. Your explanation of a software bug isn't going to win the Pulitzer Prize. Let your team write in their personal styles, and don't get hung up about grammar. As long as it's understandable and clear, you can let a few errors slip through.

Topics: Step Back When Necessary

Something that starts off as a great topic for a wiki page might not end up that way. A page that holds all the project requirements from marketing could be really great. You can link each requirement to another page that holds details about that requirement and attach documents. But it might get out of hand if someone starts adding new requirements to the list without going through change control. Then a member of the team picks up that requirement, creates the wiki subpage with the details, and starts coding it.

Step back from the wiki and use face-to-face (or at least phone conversations) when required, the same as you would do when an email exchange looks like it is getting out of hand. And don't let the wiki replace project management processes.

Irrelevance: Letting the Wiki Go Stale

People will only search the wiki for lessons learned or other information if they feel that the data they find will be up-to-date and relevant. "Lessons are not learned until they change behaviors," write Wearne and White-Hunt in *Managing the Urgent and Unexpected* (Wearne & White-Hunt, 2014). Start by changing the behavior and encouraging the team to use the wiki in the first place so that the data included is not stale.

Wiki Best Practices

Here are some good practices to consider when creating and maintaining a project wiki.

- The right length for a page is the amount of words it takes to get your message across. It's okay to have pages with a few lines or pages with hundreds of lines (although you might want to revise those long pages later if they cover several project topics).

- Use meaningful page titles. *Software Bug 24: Change Log* is good; *Fixing Bugs* is not.
- Only write about project-related information: Anything about other projects, systems, or teams should stay within the project work space for that project (an exception to this is if you have a company or team wiki that extends across multiple projects, perhaps run by the PMO).
- If you think it is worth sharing with more than one person, then share it on the wiki. Messages designed for only one person should be directed to them—pick up the phone!
- Remember that this is a professional communication channel.
- Record more than you think you need to. You'll be surprised at how much you forget over the course of a project.
- Use meaningful tags and categories.
- If someone edits one of your pages, take a look at what they've said.
- Apply self- and team-governance for spotting errors and correcting them.

Customize these practices and add your own to make your wiki deliver what you want it to. You will probably need to revisit your ground rules over time to ensure they are still relevant and tweak them accordingly.

Summary

Internal wikis run by the project team can support management activities and communication on a project. Wikis need structure in order for them to work most effectively, so the project manager setting up a wiki should consider what will be stored in it and how that information can be found later.

Optimize search features by using categories, tags, keywords, and meaningful titles. You can always edit later or add more to your taxonomies, but giving it thought in advance will save you time and make it easier for the team to find and use relevant information.

CHAPTER **11**

Managing Online Culture Shock: Risk Mitigation Strategies for Collaborating Online

If you haven't realized it by now, embarking on a collaboration tool deployment in a project environment could be fraught with difficulties. To make a change in working practices like this work, you need a supportive manager, a switched-on project sponsor, a suitable project, an enthusiastic team, and a helpful IT department. However, you could still encounter difficulties, even with all of those things in place.

This chapter will look at some of the hurdles for ensuring longevity for your software. It is not designed to put you off embarking on an initiative to adopt new technology. Rather, my aim here is to arm you with the information you will need to stop these issues from affecting your new systems. Think of this chapter as risk mitigation strategies and deploy them as you see fit in your organization.

Managing the Overload

Collaboration tools create a lot of information. You have documents and their comments, task status updates, and wiki entries that are constantly cross-referenced and revised. That's before you include the Twitter-style comments that make your phone constantly bleep with the latest updates. And it's all presented on one home page, which, while designed to give you a streamlined view of everything happening on your project, can feel busy and overwhelming.

Part of working out how best to manage online collaboration tools on your project is learning to compartmentalize and structure the constant stream of project information. Without structure, this information is useless and will not help you manage your project in a more effective way. Below are some strategies to help manage the overload.

Filtering

Your home page can show you everything that's happening on the project, or hardly anything. At the beginning of a project, it's useful to see as much as possible because you can spot where team members need support, either on their project tasks or on using the tool. As you and your team become more confident, you can switch off some of the information that you don't need to see.

You can do this by managing your alerts, as we'll see below, but you should also be conscious of the fact that you will get better at filtering out information by brain power alone.

It might not seem like it at first, but you will get better at scanning the data and filtering out what is most useful to you at any given moment. Humans are designed to process large amounts of information, and we can take in data more quickly than you think. This is all project information that you would have been storing in another method such as documents, manuals, or even in your head.

You may find that once the tool is up and running, all those messages are filling up your inbox and you *are* being overloaded. You may want to take a step back from having all that information, and that is fine. By now, people will feel confident in their use of it and there is less need for you to have an in-depth involvement in every data exchange and conversation. Cut back on the amount of data you receive.

Review the alerts you have set up and limit them to only the data that you need to see real time. If they don't need to be in real time, then set them to alert you once a day, or even weekly. If it makes you feel uncomfortable to turn them off completely, then don't. Simply direct them somewhere other than your email inbox. Set up your email software with rules to divert incoming alerts to a separate email folder or even have them go to a different email account altogether.

Then when you have the time to look through them, you can do it as a timetabled catch-up activity and focus on reading the feeds. This way, it's not something that you are trying to do on and off during the day when other tasks either take priority or provide distractions.

Once you have worked with your collaboration tool for a short time, you will be able to see which pieces of information are time-critical, and which you can be more relaxed about following up on: You will need to develop an internal "filter" to help you sift through the data and establish what is of value. Set time aside in your diary each week to review what is new on your home page or project work space, and you'll find it gets easier to hone in on the relevant data each time.

Segment the Conversations

The larger the group, the more conversation and information sharing there will be. This is not necessarily a good thing, as large groups become unwieldy and difficult to facilitate. They may not come to consensus, and they may take too long to make decisions. In short, the larger the team working on the project, the more likely it is that a collaboration tool could hinder their attempts to be efficient.

The whole group doesn't have to weigh in on every discussion. Segment the discussions by creating subteams or smaller groups so that the right people have the conversation, not the entire stakeholder body.

This can be done by providing different forums or threads for discussion. Have one place for document collaboration and another for project status updates. Use categories or tags to flag new conversations or wiki entries, so that those who are interested in participating can search for these. Use the features of the system to tailor the home pages or work spaces for each team member so they can easily see what's relevant to them today.

The point of collaboration tools is to improve information flow *between relevant people*. However, the principle of transparency is also important. You shouldn't forbid people from taking part in collaborative tasks outside their normal circle of reference. However, encourage your team to focus on those areas important to them, and don't be afraid to step in and draw a discussion to a close if you believe the team is failing to agree or move forward. After all, it's your project.

Promoting Value

Projects deliver value for their organizations and collaboration tools should provide value to the team in terms of greater efficiency, transparency, collaboration, and improved communication.

But not all chatter is a "value add."

Spend even a short amount of time on social media sites like Facebook and Twitter, and you will notice an incredible amount of exchanges that add little value to readers. This is what people are referring to when they comment that social media tools promote inefficiencies and encourage people to waste time.

Work colleagues have chatted since time began, and so it is expected that some of this will translate to the communication systems provided in the workplace. Without value in those conversations, the constant stream of data generated is just noise.

The project manager's role is to promote the right amount of chatter. Why? Because relationships are built on trust and trust comes from sharing confidences and general small talk. The balance is in allowing an amount of relationship-building chat while promoting professional conversations that help the project deliver its objectives.

This is another opportunity for the project manager to lead by example and keep too much small talk off the social media tool. The guidelines you set up as part of the deployment will help here too.

Managing the "Experts"

Have you ever sat around a meeting room table and listened to someone drone on and on? Self-proclaimed experts often want to hog the limelight, whether or not they have anything interesting or relevant to share with the wider group. If your team has a noisy "expert," you could find that your collaboration tool simply provides them with another forum in which to spout. Collaboration tools are designed to foster open communication channels, but what do you do when someone dominates the conversation?

Relevancy

Social networking sites are often perceived as ego-based systems, with the people with the largest egos contributing the most vociferously to support their own personal goals and objectives. In reality, this is not the case. There are plenty of examples of people using social media channels for collective benefit and also for the nonmonetary personal rewards from being part of an active community.

However, the view persists in some organizations that it is not appropriate to fully contribute to these sites, as it is seen as putting yourself forward in a way that is not conducive to professional business relationships. This reticence can spill over into the use of collaboration tools at work, especially if they have similar features to publicly available social networks.

If your whole team is not supported in using the tool, there is a risk that the loudest people will dominate the online discussion. And not in a good way.

Project managers need to decipher what is a relevant contribution and what is not, especially when it comes from people positioning themselves as experts. Set some ground rules about what is relevant to the discussion. You'll probably have to do this informally rather than try to codify it in a formal policy. Your systems should help you get the job done, and if you have to filter out a lot of positioning by people who like to see themselves as experts, then you will end up wasting time instead of gaining it.

You probably already know which people on the team like to dominate the conversation on the phone or in meetings. Watch out for their behavior online, and encourage them to only contribute meaningful content to the discussion. Point out when they overstep the mark or draw the conversation into irrelevant areas.

Giving a Voice to the Many

Project managers foster a project environment based on collaboration and transparent communication, valuing the input from every member of the wider stakeholder community. Collaboration tools make it easy for everyone to contribute to the discussion and to share their perspective on the issues at hand.

However, giving a voice to the many is not always a good thing. Project managers need a broad range of input to ensure a well-rounded decision-making process, but sometimes you want to be able to make the decision and move on. Debating it for weeks through the medium of two-line messages on a discussion thread is not conducive to hitting project milestones.

If this happens, step into the debate and shut it down. Just because people can contribute to the conversation doesn't mean they should, or that you have to listen. Apply the same principles as you would in a face-to-face conversation: Listen to those people who have a vested interest in influencing the outcome, weigh up the factors involved in the decision, and make the decision in a timely manner. Using online channels for communication does not mean that you give away all the control and your decision-making role. It just provides an alternative method for having discussions about the project.

While collaboration tools do make it easier for the masses to be involved in the project management process and outcomes, especially in virtual teams, they can also make it harder for some people to be adequately heard. Keep an eye on who is contributing to the project work space and recognize who is not. Ensure that everyone has the opportunity to make their point or provide their latest status update. Don't let the noisiest ones make the decisions by default.

Managing the "Always On" Culture

Enterprise collaboration systems that have features like instant messaging rely on the users being "always on." You cannot collaborate with a colleague who is not available online, so there is a reliance on your project team being online and connected. In a mobile project team where team members spend a lot of time traveling, this might not always be possible. Some of the team may be office-based, but in areas of the world that do not have reliable Internet or network connections. You can't share something with people who are not able to be on the receiving end of that sharing activity. How are you going to ensure that all project team members are able to participate in the discussions and contribute effectively?

The other major risk (or inconvenience) of being "always on" is that the lines between work and personal life become blurred. Working hours for your colleagues in Australia are sleeping hours for the European team. However, if your mobile phone is set to alert you every time someone shares a task update, your sleep could be disturbed on a regular basis. Need to join a conference call with Shanghai? No problem, as long as you can attend with the webcam switched off and stay in your pajamas.

Technology-mediated communication tools, especially those that are hosted online, make it possible for you to work on your project from wherever you are, at any time of day or night. However, just because the option is available to you doesn't mean you should do it. It is very important to manage your time and foster a culture of work/life balance in your project team.

Mobile Solutions

Mobile solutions, such as being able to access the project schedule from your phone, make it easier to manage the work/life balance. You can make the best use of your downtime when you are on the road or between meetings, and you can switch them off when you get home. Do switch them off. Very little will happen in the sleeping hours that can't wait until the next morning.

There is always the expectation on projects that sometimes you have a busy period and sometimes the work is not quite so frenetic. During the busy times, you may need to work longer hours and have your devices switched on so you can keep abreast of the latest project developments from your dispersed team. But when things reach a more manageable pace, project managers should set a good example for their teams.

Don't reply to emails late at night, as it encourages others to do so. If you find it easier or more convenient to work late at night, write your emails and save them as drafts. Then send them in the morning. This way you can live and work according to your body clock and personal preferences, without setting the expectation that this is how you want the rest of the team to work too.

Managing the Lack of Control

It might seem odd to title this section "managing the lack of control." How can you manage something when you openly admit to it not being under control?

Project managers have traditionally been the one in control of the projects. Collaborative working practices mean opening up your project management approach to enable everyone to share their knowledge and participate in the project process. That can feel like you are losing your grip on the project, even if the team's input is good quality stuff that you value.

Loosen up. Your project is not really out of control: You are facing a shift in the leadership paradigm. The old ways of leading your team are being challenged and replaced with a new way of taking control, which centers on influencing. You are fostering a collaborative workplace and encouraging your team to engage with their tasks and the project environment. That has to be a good thing, even though it might take a little while for everyone to feel comfortable about new working practices.

A collaborative team will self-organize, so you may also feel redundant. If they are so good at working out solutions and organizing their time, are you, the project manager, really required? Of course: The project manager's role is more than just telling the team what tasks to work on every day. Focus less on things that the team has under control, like who is doing what this week, and more on where your time can be better spent, like the strategic and long-term issues, project communication, and risk management. The team will need a common point of support and escalation: That's you. Promoting collaborative working practices will not make project managers redundant.

Managing Expectations

Collaboration tools will not revolutionize your project environment overnight. It takes time to affect change, and changes to working practices tend to come about slowly. It took a long time for computers to make it on to every desk. Moving to a technology-driven collaborative model for project management will take some time too, although it will be a lot faster than the advent of PCs in the workplace.

Part of the reason for this is that organizational culture is ingrained and it takes a rebranding exercise, a change in CEO, or another radical event before it starts to evolve. The age of the workforce matters as well. The older the workforce in your company and the longer the average tenure of individuals, the less likely it is they will be prepared to entertain changing their ways. Not because they eschew technological change, but because change of any sort is hard.

Think about the expectations that you hold for yourself, and don't set your sights on revolutionizing your entire organization through the introduction of a project wiki. As worthy as that objective is, recognize that organizational inertia could interfere with your plans for progress. If things go well with the wiki, introduce it to other teams or try a full-blown project collaboration tool. You can work from the ground up, carrying out a stealth operation, so once you know that your plans have been well-received, move on to something new.

The expectations of management also need to be considered. What do they believe you will achieve with team collaboration systems? As with any other project, getting clarity on what their expectations are will help you manage them throughout the deployment of your tools.

Online Etiquette

Most online etiquette (called "netiquette," which is short for "network etiquette" or, more recently, "Internet etiquette") is common sense. However, while it might be innate for the more technically literate on your team, not everyone has a grasp of how best to communicate with others online, especially in a workplace context.

Follow the communications rules that you would in real life. Be polite and courteous, and act as if you were talking to that team member in the same room, or on the phone, instead of via a computer-mediated communication tool.

There are a few extra rules for online communications:

- Don't type in ALL CAPITALS. Web users interpret this as shouting.
- If you link to a document, indicate next to the link what type of document it is. For example, you might put: *Click here to read the quality plan (.pdf)* or *Download the project charter here (.doc).* If the document has a file size of greater than 1MB, it is good practice to put the size in the brackets as well. This should stop any mobile users from unsuspectingly clicking a link and then finding they are stuck downloading a massive document that they will barely be able to read on the tiny screen anyway.
- Don't use text speak (txt spk). Spelling and grammar count toward presenting a professional image of yourself, your team, and the project online.
- Don't get side tracked. If one comment thread is about confirming scope requirements, stick to discussions about that. If you want to talk about something else, start a separate conversation thread about the new topic.
- Remember that everything entered into a public forum is public. Don't write anything that is inappropriate or unprofessional.
- Remember that everything entered into a private forum, like an instant message chat between you and other team member, is also public. Everything online can be recovered by your IT department, so don't write anything that is inappropriate or unprofessional.

- Don't use smileys, emoticons, or emojis. These are visual shorthand for the emotion and body language that is missing from written electronic communications. You'll see them more and more, but in professional communication they are considered inappropriate by most executives in most situations.

In addition to general netiquette, you could also set specific boundaries and guidelines with your team relating to your project and the way in which you want the team to operate. These can be incorporated into your team charter, or the team ground rules. Items to be included could be things like: "Respond to all comments within 24 hours" or "Always ask if it is a convenient time before initiating chat with another team member."

Creating this list of ground rules can be a collaborative effort. Involving the project team in the creation of the guidelines will also make them more responsible for policing them, and pointing out transgressions in a timely manner.

Summary

In this section, we have looked at ways to manage the change in working practices to ensure longevity for your tool deployment. The topics considered in this chapter provide a risk mitigation strategy to head off some of the hurdles of adopting technology for collaboration in a project environment.

Considering how you will manage the data overload that collaboration systems can bring will make it easier to manage the initiative as it evolves. As well as data overload, the project manager will also need to adopt strategies for managing so-called experts who dominate online conversations without adding much to the overall debate.

Collaboration tools can encourage an "always on" style of working, and this can be detrimental to the morale of the team. Try to set a good example by managing your own work/life balance and by taking time out from your project when you require it.

This hyperconnected approach to work also contributes to the perceived lack of control that some project managers feel when collaborative teamwork plays a large part in getting work done. They no longer chair meetings or conference calls, and instead hand over the conversational process to the project work space. This can be an uncomfortable position, but it is possible to manage this feeling and the practicalities around keeping control of the project.

The expectations of key stakeholders and the project team should be managed throughout the deployment of your chosen technology, and you should be aware of and manage your own expectations as well.

Finally, provide guidelines on acceptable use and online etiquette to facilitate and promote professional online communication.

CHAPTER 2

Keeping Your Project Data Secure

Data breaches are, unfortunately, more common than businesses would like and are often featured on the news. Information leakage can be costly to businesses in terms of losing the competitive advantage and also from fines for breaching data protection laws. That's why you can't just create a few user accounts and let your team loose on your new collaboration tool.

The previous chapter explained how to deal with the change of working practices that comes with moving to an online collaborative culture. This chapter continues that discussion, but focuses on the policies and processes that help a collaborative culture thrive.

This includes usage policies, access controls, and system security.

Start at the Beginning: Usage Policies

I'm willing to bet that you don't have a usage policy for meeting rooms or conference calls. There may be some informal guidelines for your company that have never been written down, such as:

- Leave the meeting room in the state that you found it
- Introduce yourself on the conference call
- Be on time for the meeting, and so on.

Collaboration tools, especially when they represent a new way of working, benefit from usage policies. The policy sets the tone around what is and is not acceptable and how the team expects to interact online.

A good starting point is your organization's social media policy. This will cover social media use inside and outside the organization (such as guidelines for staff using social networking tools) and will broadly align with the main topics you should consider for a collaboration tool usage policy.

You can also reference a Bring Your Own Device (BYOD) policy if your company has one. This states how you can use your personal devices such as your own tablet for company work. It should spell out whether you are allowed to access company data and store it on your personal device, and what the company will do if that device is lost and the company data goes along with it.

If you don't have either of those policies to draw from and link to, you may be in the 80% of companies that has a written policy covering the use and content of your emails (AMA/ePolicy Institute, 2009). This may give you some of the context relevant to a policy on collaboration tool usage.

A usage policy for your online project tools works in the same way as policies for the use of email or the Internet. It acts as a code of ethics and encourages transparency and trust between the readers and contributors.

Your collaboration tool usage policy should include:

- A definition of what counts as an electronic business record for your business (in comparison to what is "chat" or "work discussions")
- A clear, written statement of what is deemed to be acceptable use of the tool
- An explanation of what monitoring takes place (where it is legal to monitor the online activities of employees) and the consequences for employees who fail to abide by the policy
- A link to, or an explanation of, the policy about intellectual property and how this relates to internal social networks or data stored within the online collaboration tool
- A definitive statement explaining what defamation is, and links to relevant HR policies on bullying and harassment where appropriate to be absolutely clear that these behaviors are not tolerated online

- An explanation of what information is classed as "confidential" and cannot be discussed on an open internal forum, as it would be inappropriate for other employees to read this
- How employees can use their own devices for accessing the tool via apps, tablets, and so forth, and what corporate guidelines are in place regarding the loss of personal devices

Setting up a policy is not complicated. Search online for templates. Many other companies and organizations, including Imperial College London (UK) and the U.S. Department of Veterans' Affairs, have already adopted policies for the use of collaboration tools so there is plenty of material available for use as a starting point.[1] Have a look at what other companies have mandated, and see if there are any points raised in their policies that would be appropriate to adopt on your project or more widely in your organization.

Policies on Archiving

Collaboration tools add one or more data sources for your project management information. All of this data needs to be archived and filed effectively, including what is produced and stored online.

It is important to retain this information as it is part of the project history. Should anyone want to do a similar project, they may find it useful to call on the historical records to establish commonalities and avoid having to start from a blank sheet of paper.

Retention policies are also important for legal and contractual reasons. Nearly a quarter of employers have been asked to produce email as part of a lawsuit or regulatory investigation (AMA/ePolicy Institute, 2009). Add in the amount of times these data sources are called upon to

---

[1] Imperial's guidelines for collaboration tools are here: https://www.imperial .ac.uk/staff/tools-and-reference/web-guide/policies-and-guidance/ collaboration-policy/ (accessed 30 June 2015) and the VA policy is here: http://www.va.gov/vapubs/viewPublication.asp?Pub_ID=551&FType=2 (accessed 30 June 2015). There is a comprehensive database of social media policies here: http://socialmediagovernance.com/policies/ (accessed 30 June 2015).

settle contractual disputes, and you quickly start to see how important it is to be able to call on this information as and when you need it—sometimes years after the project has finished.

You need both a policy on archiving data from your collaboration tools and a means to be able to do it.

Educate Your Team

Putting policies in place is only the first step, and certainly not enough by itself. You should also make sure that employees know about them. A good way to do this is to get key members involved in researching and developing it. Policies are more likely to be adhered to if the team has input to the idea and the content.

Set up an education and monitoring program to ensure your organization is compliant with regulatory and legal guidelines. In addition, the policy should be reviewed regularly, especially as new tools are adopted by the organization.

Legal Issues

The legal issues faced by companies adopting collaboration tools are dependent on the profile of the company itself, and specifically, where it is based. If your organization has multiple offices across several continents, the legal position on storing employee data (such as name, contact details, photo, and other profile information, for example, on your wiki author pages) will be influenced by the laws pertaining to the geographies in which you work.

Employees in the United States, for example, have no reasonable expectation of privacy when using a company's computer systems. In the United Kingdom, employees do have a reasonable right to privacy, although monitoring of the use of computer systems is allowed, as long as employees are aware that it is happening.

The issue of where data is stored is particularly relevant for project management applications hosted in the cloud. As this type of software is not stored on your corporate servers, it could be hosted anywhere. Reputable cloud providers will answer all your questions about data protection. Take advice from your corporate legal and IT teams if you have any concerns.

Figure 12.1:   Elements of a secure social media system.

Addressing Security Concerns

Security should be built into your collaboration tool deployment project from the beginning: It's not something you should think about afterward. The five security elements of collaboration tools are shown in Figure 12.1 and are discussed in more detail below.

1. Access Control

Most collaboration tools are accessible to everyone within the organization, and some even allow access for trusted third parties, outsourcing partners, and clients. It is typical that while the tool is available to all, project data is limited to the team who needs to see it—but you may need to set up smaller project teams or groups within the system in order to partition that data away from everyone else.

The devolved communication model (which takes the responsibility for managing all project communications away from the project and puts it in the hands of the project team), presents some security concerns. It is a lot easier to have confidential discussions about project progress or corporately-sensitive projects by email, or in a meeting room with the door shut. Put those conversations online for the whole company to see and you could end up with a communications problem.

There is a risk, albeit small, that someone will take the project-specific information shared on the system, and distribute it elsewhere, in a public forum. Whether this is an innocent activity or one with a more sinister agenda, sharing company information outside of company walls is a potential corporate risk. All it takes is for someone in a different department to stumble across your project work space or an unsecure document and write about it on their own personal blog. "I found out something interesting today: My company is working on XYZ." Suddenly, the news about a forthcoming new product that will give your company a competitive edge has been leaked to the outside world.

Policies, as we saw above, are one way to avoid situations like this, but in practice, it can be hard to get that level of engagement and security from staff outside your core user group, especially as the shared values of transparency and openness seem to go against security and confidentiality. It can be a difficult balance, especially for new employees or those who have not come across this sort of workplace tool before.

Managing access controls to the collaboration tools is a good way to manage the flow of data within the organization. The focus for your project team should be on using the tools to collaborate more effectively and establish a positive working environment for project delivery, not firefighting the fact that someone in the Australian office has gotten a hold of your project plan and let it slip to the customer that you are three weeks behind schedule.

Access controls normally mean giving the users distinct usernames and passwords, and making the tools available only to those people who log in. This means that only people who have a username and password are able to see the data in the tool, and as project manager, you can monitor who is given access. You might want to delegate this to the PMO or a project support officer. Develop a process for requesting access to the tool. Ideally, access should not be refused without good reason, as part of the rationale for shifting work online is to share information. However, never hesitate to block access if it is inappropriate, or if your project team is working with data that needs to remain confidential or secure.

Similarly, ensure that any nondisclosure or confidentiality agreements you have in place with third parties, contractors, and other partners includes specific mention of information held in enterprise collaboration tools. Third parties may require usernames and passwords to access these tools, and as most implementations will be hosted in the cloud, there should be no reason why this is not possible. Follow the same guidelines as you would for any permanent member of staff: Share the relevant policy with the third party, ask for compliance, and issue a distinct username and password per person.

In addition, you might want to limit which areas within your online project work space the third party can see. For example, contractors should only be able to see information that relates to their ability to do their job. You'll want to keep budget information and staff rates confidential, along with any contracts or terms that relate to other suppliers.

You can, of course, refuse access completely for third parties, at least until you have grasped how it works and have identified any potential security risks.

2. Back Ups

Data held in your collaboration tool is still business data that should be treated as such. Your emails are probably backed up securely, as is the rest of the data stored on any shared file servers or network drives that you use regularly at work. Discussion threads, wiki pages, and other data streams are of a similar degree of importance to those documents backed up elsewhere. Make sure you have a process in place by which information in the collaboration tool can be backed up securely.

If you are using cloud computing services (software-as-a-service), then the responsibility for backup will rest with the vendor. Make sure that you are happy with the level of backup they can provide for you and that you have confidence that, should the worst happen and the company stop trading for whatever reason, that you can retrieve the information you need.

It's also worth exploring the business continuity plans that the vendor has in place. If you recognize that your use of the tool is essential to keep the organization working, then you'll want the confidence of knowing what happens in the event of a disaster.

3. Audit Trails

No one should have anonymous access to your collaboration tools. No one should have a generic account. Generic accounts are ones where a team shares the same username and password like *accounts@mycompany.com*. While these do have their place, they make it difficult to find out who did what at any given moment.

Individual usernames and passwords mean that it is possible to track who posted or accessed what information. This gives you a complete audit trail.

Not all software has the capability to store audit trails. Instead of a complete history, for example, you might only get the name of the last person to access that record, and the time they did so. This might be adequate for your needs—or you might not be bothered about storing an audit trail at all. Your IT security team can advise you on corporate policies about audit trails and what, if anything, should be stored.

It is good practice to let the people who are using the software know that it has an audit trail facility (if it does) so they are aware that their interactions with the system can be tracked if necessary.

4. Abuses of the System

In a global survey of over 100 companies, the majority of businesses reported having to deal with social media misuse. More than 70% of businesses have taken disciplinary action against an employee in relation to misusing social media (Proskauer, n. d.). With over 80% of companies reporting that the misuse of social media is going to be more of an issue in the future, this is not a trend that is going away.

Email is not exempt from bad behavior either: Nearly 90% of respondents in another survey reported that they had sent "jokes, gossip, rumors, or disparaging remarks" via their work email to an external party (AMA/ePolicy Institute, 2009).

While it isn't palatable and you hope it won't happen, it's unrealistic to think that the collaboration tools you set up at work will be free from abuse. Logic tells us that you are likely to get fewer instances of system abuse on a tool that is designed for workplace collaboration and is, therefore, monitored by management, than on personal Facebook sites, but the risk is still there.

Abusing the system like this is unacceptable workplace behavior and if you become aware of it, use the existing management and human resources processes to deal with this as a disciplinary action.

It is far better to avoid this situation by making it very clear, through the use of a policy, what is and is not acceptable behavior. You can also introduce tools that allow other users to flag inappropriate content, although in a small team, hopefully this can be tackled through monitoring behavior rather than policing each other's interactions online.

5. Unauthorized Software

The final security concern relating to collaboration software is the risk that team members want to try out and adopt different products. Many online collaboration tools offer free trials and there is nothing wrong with testing different products until you find one that meets your needs (in fact, that's exactly what you should do).

However, the final choice and adoption of an enterprise solution should be done in a considered way. Find out what process is in place for software approval and follow the IT guidelines about procuring new tools. This is essential for the long-term success of your system because without the support (and knowledge) of your IT team, you could be creating more difficulties for yourself later. If the app stops working or requires an upgrade, who will support it? By now it has become a critical way of collaborating and without it, your project team's productivity will fall. IT support teams are reluctant to take responsibility for fixing software they did not approve or install. More seriously, downloading software in an unapproved fashion can open up the company to vulnerabilities such as viruses and other security threats.

The use of unauthorized, uncontrolled software should be strongly discouraged. Make your project team aware of this. If they have any requests for additional tools, go through the proper channels.

Summary

Enterprise implementations require a robust approach to the security of corporate data and a full suite of enforced policies to ensure confidentiality is maintained across a diverse user group.

Identify and address the security concerns that are likely to face your collaboration tool deployment project and work with your IT team and other corporate teams such as the legal department to establish clear guidelines. Inform users how the system will be monitored and what action will be taken if the tools are abused.

Your approach to security should be designed into the tool from the first use, and should not be something considered as an afterthought once the product is up and running.

The Bigger Picture

Part 3 looks outside of your project to the wider online world. It examines how you can build a personal brand and professional credibility through online collaboration with your peers, using collaboration tools outside of your own company's environment.

It also looks forward to assess some of the future trends in online collaboration that will affect working practices and project management in years to come.

It includes the following chapters:

- Chapter 13: Building Personal Online Credibility
- Chapter 14: Conclusions: The Future of Work

Building Personal Online Credibility

Collaboration tools at work give you the opportunity to build credibility with your team and stakeholders. You can extend this more widely to your industry peers, professional bodies, and potential employers when you use publicly available collaboration tools and social networks.

Credibility is part of your personal brand. In an increasingly competitive marketplace having a solid personal brand is something that can set you apart from other project managers.

There are plenty of opportunities to create and foster your personal brand online. Social media tools give you a lot of outlets to put forward your best professional self online for recruiters and colleagues to see. This chapter takes the idea of online collaborative and social tools for professional use further than your immediate project environment and covers how you can use social media to build a successful career.

Getting Started

Most of the career benefits of being online come from connecting with other people, whether they are other project management practitioners from whom you can learn and share experiences, or potential employers. As we have seen, online tools are very social and they facilitate connections between people. The principles of using collaboration tools in the workplace to improve project performance are the same as using social media in your own time to learn new skills or get a new job. The only difference is likely to be that at work you use such tools in a way that supports your corporate approach to information security. When you use social media to build an online presence for yourself, you are doing it in a much more public setting.

Social networking is the variant of social media that refers to using the Internet to connect with other people. There are plenty of websites out there to facilitate meeting people online—and we're not talking about Internet dating. Facebook, Bebo, Xing, Ning, MySpace, LinkedIn: The choices are dazzling, so where should a professional project manager start?

At the time of writing, the predominant business social network is LinkedIn. LinkedIn is used by 92% of project managers, so unless you are starting out in your career, it's likely you are already on there (Scott, 2013). You can also find a large project management presence on the social networking site, Ning.[1] PMI also has an online public community with discussion forums, blogs, polls, and the ability to connect to others. Find it at www.projectmanagement.com. You do not have to be a PMI member to join.

If you are just getting started, ask your colleagues which social networks they are part of. Alternatively, do an Internet search for the major commentators in your industry and see where they are hanging out online. The big networks might not be the most appropriate: If you work in a very small or specialized industry, it could be better for you to join a network specializing in that. You can join more than one network, but don't overstretch yourself. Join too many and you will find it hard to keep them all up-to-date, and you will dilute the benefits that you would have gotten from participating regularly in just the one.

Once you have chosen which network to join, sign up for an account. The next stage will be creating your online profile, which is the first step to being able to showcase your abilities and skills online.

The Way We Work Now

Using social media is a choice. However, what was considered innovative three years ago is now commonplace. While you don't have to set up a LinkedIn profile, social tools are becoming more and more of an expected part of your professional tool kit. Consider what message you are sending if you don't have an online presence.

---

[1] Ning is a social networking platform that brings together groups with a common interest. The Professional Project Managers Networking Group (PPMNG) on Ning can be accessed at http://www.projectmanagers.net/

Creating an Online Profile

In the *Journal of New Communications Research*, David Phillips writes:

> Way back in the 1990s, it was evident that many people online had several different online personalities. Even today, most of us have a number of email addresses, where a Hotmail or Gmail account serves different purposes than a work email account. Our Facebook profile differs from our LinkedIn profile. . . People seek society in different groups, different types of groups, and for (sometimes convergent) different purposes and different selves (Phillips, 2008).

Different profiles serve different purposes. Consider having two online profiles in different tools: one for your friends and one as an outwardly-facing professional profile. As Phillips says, Facebook and LinkedIn serve different audiences. Facebook is a good tool to use for connecting with your friends. LinkedIn, however, is a professional business network aimed at putting business people in touch with colleagues who share similar interests.

Multiple Profiles on the Same Site

Check the terms of service for each social network site you sign up for. You may find it breaches the terms of service to create multiple accounts. If you are worried about sharing more personal items with your colleagues, such as photos of your holidays on Facebook where you are also connected to your staff, then check your security privileges. It is possible—on Facebook, at least—to change the sharing status of any of your updates to only share them with the people you want. This does rely on you remembering to do that for every item, otherwise that picture of you swimming with dolphins might reach a wider audience than you expected.

All social media sites ask you to create a personal profile. This is a short description of yourself, often with a photo, to enable others on the site to get an insight into your skills and interests. Twitter expects users to be able to do this in 160 characters, reflecting the short communication style. LinkedIn, however, is at the opposite extreme and will allow you to enter a complete educational and career history.

Profiles allow you to link to other people and for others to link to you: This is the "networking" part of a social network. Different tools call this different things. In LinkedIn terminology, you are "connected" to someone. On Facebook, they become your "friend" and on Twitter, they become a "follower." On ProjectManagement.com, they join your "network." It all means the same thing; you have linked to them in some way. Think of it as a virtual exchange of business cards.

A strong online profile is important for project managers attempting to set themselves apart from the crowd online. This is especially useful when competing for jobs, but also for creating a professional appearance. Your profile can help establish you as an expert in work breakdown structures, earned value management, engineering project management, or any other specialism that you wish to highlight. It can also provide subsidiary information that you can't find space for on your CV or résumé.

Think about the image you want to portray: a professional, credible project manager. Here are some profile pointers:

- How do you want people to contact you? Set your contact preferences carefully if you don't want random strangers instant messaging you during the working day. Allowing people to contact you by email is the easiest to manage.
- Make a point of saying that you can provide additional information and references if required. It is not necessary to list everything and publish your references online.
- Don't give out personal details like your address or date of birth.
- Be wary of updating your status to reflect the fact that you are away on leave or out of the office on a business trip. Personal security should always be at the forefront of your mind.
- Think about what other people would like to know about you and your career. A list of your favorite books (although I have been asked that at an interview) or favorite foods is not likely to be of interest to people contacting you for professional purposes. Your background in engineering projects is likely to be relevant.
- Having said that, it is worth providing a few details to give other users a flavor of your personality, like a short list of hobbies or other interests.

- Consider who you want to be able to access your details. Most social networking sites offer a limited view of your profile to people who are not connected to you, and your full profile is only available to those whom you have approved as friends or connections.
- You don't have to use your real name on social networking sites (although some sites mandate this), but if you want to be taken seriously, you should.
- Be truthful! Accuracy matters, as it is very easy to find out when someone has exaggerated or lied on their profile.

Photos

Social media sites also encourage uploading a profile picture or photo, sometimes called an avatar. This is normally very small on the screen, so think about what picture to use. A headshot works well. Posed corporate headshots of the type that grace your company's annual report are a bit staid for social media sites. Photos that look like they have been taken with a selfie stick or snapped on your phone in front of a mirror are too informal. Something that looks relaxed, but that still shows you as professional (no swimming costumes or Santa hats) would be better.

Still not sure? Have a look at your manager's photo or those of your colleagues to get an idea of what is acceptable.

Nothing is Private!

The Internet has a long memory, and privacy is a hot topic when it comes to sharing your personal information. Within your company's firewall, the data that you share on project collaboration tools can be considered as secure as possible, baring attacks by hackers. However, nothing you put on the Internet outside of your company's environment is truly private, so having a personal profile on another site doesn't mean that your work colleagues will never see it. Facebook, for example, does have strict privacy controls, but setting them up can be awkward and many people don't bother. The disadvantage here is that people who seek you out, maybe as a result of social networking through another site, will be able to see your personal data—and that could work against you if you are not careful.

The rule of thumb is: Never put anything online you wouldn't want your boss to see.

The Risk of Digital Sharecropping

Digital sharecropping is where your content—your online résumé, photographs, and other assets that build up your online profile—is fully hosted on someone else's web real estate.

Say, for example, that LinkedIn closed down tomorrow. Would you exist online anywhere else, or would you have to build up your online reputation from scratch again? What if Facebook changed their policy and your small business page was deleted?

Many of the benefits of having an online profile come from participating on forums and shared sites, but if you are serious about building an online reputation that you can totally control, it is worth investigating creating your own website or blog. That would give you digital real estate in your own name that you can manage yourself without having to rely on a social network.

The Risks of Being Online

Graham Cluley is a Senior Technology Consultant at Sophos and an expert in computer viruses and spam. He's acknowledged around the world as one of the industry's thought leaders and writes an award-winning blog. And he was the victim of a bizarre identity theft on Facebook.

An unscrupulous user created some controversial groups on Facebook and started posting discussion topics using inflammatory language. The openness and ease of interaction with others on social networking sites is a benefit to most users, but is also a risk, as not everyone plays by the community's rules. This user needed a photo for his personal profile—and he chose one of Cluley that he found online.

So it started with a picture of Cluley on a profile that wasn't his own, and some inflammatory remarks. Another user on Facebook recognized Cluley from the picture and announced the "identity" of the person behind the comments. Once the Facebook community thought they knew who was to blame, they mobilized against Cluley, who was on holiday in Cambodia at the time.

Cluley was bombarded with emails and received death threats against himself and his family. The Internet connection wasn't good in Cambodia, but he did find out what was going on and asked Facebook to step in and remove the abuse from its site. Facebook was slow to respond, advising Cluley to contact the police. Fortunately, journalists picked up the story and Facebook finally closed down the discussion groups and removed the unfounded accusations against Cluley.

This is an extreme example of the perils of being online. It shouldn't put you off from joining a social networking site, but it does highlight the need to monitor and maintain your online presence.[2]

Social Media for Continuing Professional Development

Many professional development organizations require credential holders to undergo continuous professional development. Social media sites can help with that.

Consult the guidelines from your professional organization and find out exactly what counts toward your ongoing professional development. Self-directed learning normally qualifies for part of your professional development requirement.

There are podcast providers that offer professional development credits. You can keep up-to-date with industry news on blogs. Product manufacturers offer video clips and articles about their products to help you become more efficient at using project management tools.

Even if you can't use project management-related social media tools toward maintaining your credentials, they still offer a great deal of professional development information. You will find podcasts and educational blogs covering all aspects of project, program, and risk management, aimed at beginners and experts. Given the thousands of blogs out there, you will have to sift through what is available before you find something that strikes a chord with you. The Appendix has a list of online resources you can use as a starting point.

The groups feature in LinkedIn allows you to ask questions of your peers and participate in discussions about project management. This collaborative aspect of social media provides a lot of opportunities to learn more about the role and responsibilities of a project manager.

---

[2] You can read Cluley's account of what happened and how he addressed it on his blog: Cluley, S. (2008, April 28). Facebook, trolls, temples and death threats. *Sophos.com*. Retrieved from http://www.sophos.com/blogs/gc/g/2008/04/28/facebook-trolls-and-death-threats/

Make a list of your favorite sites and visit them regularly. You are bound to learn something new, hear about an opportunity to collaborate on something you would find interesting, or find an opportunity to pass on your experience to someone else.

The Power of Twitter

To give you an example of how powerful and useful online tools can be, here's how a conversation on Twitter unfolded.

Kathy posted a comment on my blog asking for recommendations for a project management collaboration tool with a 60-day free trial. I took to Twitter to widen the discussion and asked my followers for suggestions.

Within hours, I had responses from the community including the one you can see in Figure 13.1. Stas Zlobinski (@Agency_PM) got in touch to recommend a tool he had used, but unfortunately it didn't meet the 60-day free trial criteria. He linked the website in the tweet and the company, Active Collab, got in touch to offer a 90-day trial.

Elizabeth Harrin @pm4girls · Jul 29
Kathy is looking for an easy online PM tool, with 60 days free or cheap. Share your recommendation here: pm4girls.elizabeth-harrin.com/2014/07/ppm-pr...
Thanks #pmot

Expand   Reply   Delete   Favorite   More

Agency PM @Agency_PM · 19h
.@pm4girls I used this tool with good success. activecollab.com It's a 30 day free trial, not 60, but it's worth it.

Expand   Reply   Retweet   Favorite   More

activeCollab @activecollab · 13h
@Agency_PM We can make it 90 ;) Create a demo and email support@activecollab.com for an extension cc @pm4girls

Expand   Reply   Retweet   Favorite   More

Agency PM @Agency_PM · 7h
@activecollab nice! @pm4girls there you go. It's a great offer.

2:51 AM - 31 Jul 2014 · Details

💬 Hide conversation   ↩ Reply 🔁 Retweet ★ Favorite ••• More

Figure 13.1:   How a Twitter conversation unfolded.

I don't know whether Kathy took up the offer, but I feel this example illustrates the knowledge sharing and collaboration that can go on through social networks when you tap into the discussion.

Social Recruiting: The Job Search Moves Online

Social sites are now hot real estate for recruiters. A survey by Jobvite[3] shows that 93% of recruiters use or plan to use social media for their recruitment campaigns. That covers everything from pushing alerts to qualified people in their staff's social networks through automated tools to putting job ads on LinkedIn.

The influence of social recruitment also means that fewer jobs are offered and filled through traditional job boards. Your network becomes a way for job offers to reach you and for you to help your employer fill positions. The challenge then relates to how you can adequately increase your network to tap into that source of job adverts.

Social networking helps with this in the following ways:

- It increases the number of references and advocates in your professional circle of influence
- It provides a larger referral base for new career opportunities
- It provides a larger resource base for assistance and advice
- It gives you the opportunity to capitalize on your personal brand by building and promoting your professional image online

You could get all of these benefits from face-to-face networking, but using online tools makes it easier to connect with more people for less effort and allows you to mingle with project managers in other countries, which you couldn't easily do face-to-face or on the phone.

Social networking sites do have their limitations. For example, they tend to work better for contractors or consultants looking for short-term work. If you are in the market for a permanent entry-level role, you will have to look harder to get any leads.

---

[3] http://web.jobvite.com/FY15_SEM_2014SocialRecruitingSurvey_LP.html Accessed 3 August 2015.

Equally, it is easier to job hunt on a social networking site if you are *not* currently working. Changing your profile to reflect that you are looking for a new job could alert your current employer to the fact that you are about to quit, so if you are currently in a job, be careful about how you do your online job seeking.

The social aspect of sites like LinkedIn means that there is nearly always someone online to respond to questions quickly. Discussion groups are good places to find general career advice for free, which can be useful if you are looking to change the focus of your career or branch out into a new industry. Ask a question and let the experts reply to you with the answer. People will soon get tired of someone who asks, but does nothing to contribute to the wider discussion, so take the time to comment on other discussion threads and share some of your own expertise as well.

Social networking is like any other face-to-face business networking event. If you attend a conference and collect a lot of business cards, which you then throw away, you have wasted the opportunity to build relationships with those you have met. Online networking is the same: Just having a presence online doesn't mean that job offers will start flooding your way. Once your details are out there, you should work at keeping your profile up-to-date and make an effort to connect with other people. Think about building relationships instead of just building your network.

Help With Interview Preparation

Aside from hunting down your next career move, the Internet can also help you prepare for an interview. Reading a company's public blogs can help you understand what working for them would really be like. Their annual report, press releases, and other information available online give you the chance to evaluate the company before you apply. Check out the company's social profiles on Facebook and Twitter as well.

Regularly click on the corporate blogs of the companies that you particularly want to work for. You might come across some information about new initiatives or projects that convinces you that now is the time to send off your CV or résumé. Look for clues about who might be recruiting or working on interesting projects. If nothing else, this will give you some material when the interviewer asks you, "Do you have any questions for us?" It's far more impressive to speak eloquently about what you know of their latest projects and challenges than to respond with, "No, you've covered everything."

Job Hunting Online

Web-based tools offer a good platform for job seeking project managers to put more information about themselves online and build a personal brand to attract and inform recruiters. However, this works both ways: You can also use social media tools like business networking sites to connect with people who are most likely to be in need of your skills and services.

"When a job seeker is in the market for a new job, nothing beats the strength of their own personal network in helping them find the ideal job," says Lindsay Scott, Director of Arras People, a specialist project management recruitment consultancy. "More importantly, it tends to be a less stressful way of finding a new position."

Social networking sites are good ways to build a professional network online and many project managers use them to keep in touch with colleagues from previous jobs or people they have met face-to-face at conferences and events.

Scott has these tips for joining an online network:

- Take time to create your public profile.
  The profile is not a CV or résumé, and therefore shouldn't just list your career history. The profile should be short and to the point, but enticing enough for people to want to contact you and strike up a networking opportunity. Successful profiles tend to focus on a particular project management specialism, high profile program or project you've managed, prominent organizations worked in, and other project management groups you might also be a member of.
- Make it clear on your profile what your objective is in joining the network.
  If your primary focus is job seeking, say so. Make it clear on the profile what you are interested in and what you're looking for. This should help cut down on approaches which are irrelevant to your needs.
- Put in some effort.
  Start to build up individual links to others that share similar skills, backgrounds, or experiences or those that offer skills that you don't currently have. While you are looking for the dream job, you could be picking up additional skills, advice, and tips from others along the way.

- Be truthful.
  Don't be economical with the truth. Some job seekers have a tendency to be a little too enthusiastic when writing the profile, which could come back to bite them, especially as all their peers and colleagues will be able to read it.
- Think quality over quantity.
  It doesn't matter that you have 600 contacts! Ten carefully selected contacts would be much easier to manage and would probably value the relationship more, helping you to be much more productive in reaching your goal.

Being Credible

Unfortunately, it is easy to build fake profiles online. Just because you say you have a raft of credentials and two decades of experience doesn't mean that you actually do. Part of building your personal brand—the most important part—is being as credible as possible in everything you do online.

Credibility online is sometimes called a "net rep" as in "Internet reputation." Just as you have a reputation at work for being a great project manager (I hope), being active online will give you a reputation, and of course, you want this to be as positive as possible. Building a positive, professional reputation online is done in exactly the same way as you would do it offline. Adhere to the same ethical codes that guide the rest of your project management activity. If someone asks you a question, reply. If someone responds to your request for information, thank them for their time. It's not complicated, but these little exchanges will help create a professional impression.

A professional impression is important to your current employer as well. In a study by CareerBuilder, 39% of hiring managers reported that spending time on personal social media accounts during office hours was a major blocker for giving someone a promotion (CareerBuilder.com, 2015).

Jobvite's 2014 Social Recruiting Survey[4] says that 55% of recruiters have reconsidered a candidate based on their social media profiles and

---

[4] Jobvite. Retrieved from http://web.jobvite.com/FY15_SEM_2014SocialRecruiting Survey_LP.html

that 61% of those reconsiderations have been negative. Illegal drug references, sexual posts, and poor spelling and grammar top the list of reasons why employers change their minds about candidates. Details about volunteer experience and charity donations can change a recruiter's mind the other way: 65% of hiring managers say that puts candidates in a more positive light.

You can also build your credibility in the project management space through creating your own content. You could set up a personal blog to share your own experiences of and skills in project management. Blogging is a useful thing to have on your CV or résumé, as it shows that you are committed to fostering good communications through building relationships with your audience, and once your blog gets a core of regular readers and other people start to hear about your writing, it will show that you are considered an expert in your field.

Blogging takes a lot of commitment, as an out-of-date blog or one that appears to be rarely updated will not help frame you as an expert in the field. Here are some alternative, lower-commitment activities that you could do to build your online reputation:

- Contribute to discussions on social networking groups. Ask and answer questions. Try to avoid commenting on very controversial topics, but if you do give an opinion, do it in a measured way.
- Contribute project templates to document-based online communities, or sites that allow you to upload files.
- Comment on other people's blogs, both in the project management arena and on sites that reflect the industry you operate in, for example, financial services or engineering.
- Share articles you have written on multi-author sites or on LinkedIn. This still lets you reach a wide audience with your ideas while limiting the effort involved in maintaining a blog.

The Company You Keep

The people who form your online network are also part of how you will be judged online. Forget connecting to celebrities from your professional profile. Ideally, you want your professional connections to be exactly that—people with whom you have worked in a professional capacity.

By all means, connect to people who look interesting or to whom you would want to build relationships with, but do think carefully before befriending them online. Other people will check you out before connecting with you, so do the same.

Pay Attention to the Little Things

Everything about how you relate to other people online can help build a professional, personal brand, including your email signature. An email signature is the bit of text that appears at the bottom of your messages. Many companies mandate how this should appear for corporate email accounts, and it probably includes your name, job title, contact details, the company website address, and possibly a corporate logo. Your personal email account can be set up in the same way.

The email signature on your personal email account doesn't have to be as long or convoluted as your corporate email account, but it can be used to your advantage, especially if you are job hunting or contacting someone in your social network. Web-based (like Hotmail, Gmail, and Yahoo) and client-based (like Outlook and Lotus Notes) email systems can be configured to include a signature. You could even create templates with different signature information for different purposes. For example, a signature with all your contact information for recruiters and another one with just a link to your LinkedIn profile (or equivalent) for everyone else.

Summary

Social media tools provide the opportunity to create a personal brand online. The first step in creating your professional, personal brand is to have a presence on a social networking site. Have separate profiles for your work life and your personal life, but be aware that nothing online is ever truly private, so don't post anything to the web that would embarrass you or your employer.

The web is also a great place to find career advice. Project management discussion groups on social networking sites provide the chance to ask and answer questions. Blogs and podcasts cover all aspects of project management and are useful learning tools for continuing professional development.

Finally, if you are in the market for a new job, your social network can help with your search. While the information about you online is not the most important thing that recruiters take into account, they do use the web to find additional information on candidates. Make sure that what recruiters read about you is the professional image that you wish to portray.

CHAPTER 14

Conclusions: The Future of Work

The way we work as project managers, as teams, and as leaders is changing constantly. Today, the pace of change seems almost unmanageable, and yet, we must manage it or find ourselves and our businesses obsolete. So, where to next for the technical trends around collaboration and teamwork that will affect how project managers operate in the years to come?

Predicting anything to do with technology is difficult. It becomes increasingly difficult in a world where everyone can contribute their ideas, and where the barriers to entry for innovative new software is so low. Simon Moore, in his book, *Strategic Project Portfolio Management*, uses the fax as an example of how difficult it is to predict the future. Email didn't wipe out fax use, although many people predicted it would. Even though using a fax machine is more expensive and time consuming than email, fax machines are still used. They are being edged out by software that allows for secure and reliable digital signatures, but you'll still find them, tucked away in the corner of many offices. Moore predicts that the fax machine will one day soon become obsolete, but reminds us that it is notoriously difficult to predict the timing of technology change (Moore, 2010).

I made some predictions of my own in an earlier version of this book, *Social Media for Project Managers*. Time to hold myself accountable: Let's see how accurate these were.

Traditional project management tools will take on the features and functionality provided by social media tools.

Yes. Project management software today does include social collaboration features on a more routine basis. This allows companies to consolidate their tools and achieve better compliance for security and integration.

Gartner's 2015 Magic Quadrant report into project and portfolio software applications (Stang, Handler, & Jones, 2015) concludes that this is happening in four ways:

- Vendors are relying on basic communication tools such as discussions and email integration.
- Vendors are partnering with social networking and collaboration software firms such as Salesforce's Chatter.
- Vendors are developing native social collaboration features as part of their core product.
- Vendors are buying companies that provide that capability and incorporating it into their offering, such as Microsoft's acquisition of Yammer, or Planview's acquisition of Projectplace.

Project management software portals will consolidate behind the scenes social tools and present a common interface to the user.

No. I haven't seen this happen, but there are greater connections between systems through application program interfaces (APIs) and third-party tools that allow for synchronization and sharing of data. My current thoughts on technical interoperability are discussed below.

Project managers will have to switch tools at some point.

This is probably the case. The market is still immature with many new products being introduced and bought as companies consolidate and expand. It is highly likely that project managers still face the risk of investing significant time and effort in implementing one collaboration suite only to find that they have to move to another, perhaps enterprise solution, in a few years.

Project managers deploying social and collaborative systems today will have to keep a careful eye on the fortunes of their supplier and act quickly should the market change.

Biometric scanning will be incorporated into the next generation of tools.

This isn't widespread. While fingerprint recognition lets you log in to Apple hardware without a passcode, retina and fingerprint scanning for logging into online systems is still not common. Most online social, collaboration, and project management systems still rely on usernames and passwords or two-factor authentication, probably because it is cheap and easy to implement and there is, as yet, not sufficient user demand.

Teams will become less reliant on hierarchy as a result of flexibility in the workplace.

Yes. Both formally and informally, there is a growing acceptance of flexible working practices and non-hierarchical methods. In other words, we have moved even further away from the old command and control style of management that we were seeing six years ago.

This hasn't changed the requirement for having a project manager on a team. Self-managed teams still benefit from a project manager to facilitate the completion of a project, but they are internally motivated to get the job done, and to work in a more open, collaborative way.

There are still many project managers who may find this uncomfortable, especially if they were used to being able to dictate the way in which the team and project function. "The project manager becomes a social architect who understands the interaction of organizational and behavioral variables, inspires team members, facilitates the work process, and provides overall project leadership for developing multi-disciplinary task groups into unified teams, hence fostering a climate conducive to involvement, commitment, and conflict resolution," writes Hans Thamhain, in his essay, "The Future of Team Leadership in Complex Project Environments" (Thamhain, 2009). This type of working is especially relevant to virtual teams, who have to build trust in others—sometimes people they have never met—in order to deliver to the business objectives.

The makeup of teams will continue to evolve.

Yes. We've seen a greater shift toward partnership, crowdsourcing, and user-driven contributions. The inclusion of external partners in project teams, as more companies adapt to the requirements of globalization and competition, is the norm. Tools are recognizing this, with functionality that offers limited views of the project data to third parties.

The Net Generation, the digital natives of our society, will drive the demand for social and collaboration tools.

Yes, although perhaps the change has been more slow than anticipated. Some industries haven't embraced the social revolution as quickly as others, but it will continue to change as those millennials make it to senior management positions. For this generation, these tools are not gadgets or novelties; they are a way of life. Having grown up in a digital economy, we should continue to expect their background and working preferences to influence project management and wider business.

A project software firm I was consulting with asked how they could better position their product to attract project managers in more traditional industries. I responded that I didn't think the industry itself needed to change: The people holding those project management positions would change and it would be the profile of the team members who drove and demanded new technology.

Project management training will move out of the classroom and focus on soft skills.

Yes. The past few years have seen a significant shift away from technical project management skills to the acknowledgment that projects are all about people, and perhaps, it's time we started training our project leaders in soft skills.

Classroom-based training is still incredibly popular, but it feels like there are more quality, approved, online training options.

The focus on "being green" will support virtual working and collaboration tools due to reduced travel costs.

No. While green project management is still at the forefront of many people's minds, the environmental aspects of flexible working are not publicized as the reason why companies adopt flexible working practices or collaboration tools. The economic position over the last few years has driven down margins, and smarter, cheaper ways of working have been, I would suggest, in response to reducing cost, rather than reducing the impact on the environment. Where the two objectives align, this is a happy accident.

The questions about the green credentials of cloud computing and the "always on" culture have yet to be answered. Huge server farms sited offshore may cut your immediate utility bills, saving on power and the cost of running the air conditioning in a server room. But these costs are just redistributed to the SaaS provider. What are the green credentials of these server farms? These are the ethical implications for managing from the cloud. In addition to this, manufacturers still have to ensure the smallest possible carbon footprint for devices that are going to be used 24 hours a day to receive project updates.

We will see an increasing use of mobile devices connected to the Internet and the software to run on them.

Yes, although my observation is anecdotal. An informal survey of software vendors today shows that many of them have responded to consumer demand for apps. However, the growing overhead of keeping apps up-to-date and available on multiple platforms may prove too much.

The alternative is fully web-responsive websites. Many companies, pre-warned by Google of an algorithm change in April 2015, adapted their websites to be mobile-friendly. This was as a response to the growing numbers of users accessing websites on a mobile device. A mobile-efficient web theme sees the screen wrap elegantly to the size of the screen, making it possible and practical to browse the web on the go.

Project management software traditionally has relied on a mouse and keyboard for data entry, often with multiple points of data entry on a single screen. Windows users can right click for even more options. Mobile-friendly websites and apps will have to overcome this by introducing features that make it possible to actually use the software effectively and not just view it from a tablet or smartphone.

Social media and enterprise collaboration tools will make more of the notion of "presence."

No. Presence is a concept that shows who is online at any one time and how they want to be communicated with. For example, someone on a conference call may be willing to be interrupted by instant messages, but someone preparing a detailed document may set their contact preferences to "none."

Presence technology hasn't taken off significantly and hasn't evolved in the mainstream any further than relying on the user to update their notification settings. It could pick up clues from the user's location or activity and update their status directly, but it seems we are a ways off from that right now.

Geo-tagging, or geolocation, is related to presence and refers to being able to tag blog posts, photos, and other social media content with where you are. The business applications of this, aside from being able to offer customers discounts if you notice they are in your area, seem unexplored at the moment with regard to project teams and collaboration.

Looking Forward: Seven Future Trends

Having explored the evolution of technology trends over the past few years, let's now look forward. There are some emerging themes in both project management and in social and collaborative technologies that warrant a watching brief for those interested in how the two fields interrelate.

1. Project Analytics

Data is a differentiator. Companies that can capture what customers buy, like, and use can interrogate that data to provide insights that help them stay ahead of the curve. Big data is the term given to the storage and analysis of workplace data for the purpose of creating meaningful management information.

The data from collaboration and project management tools is a subset of all this data. Real-time project analytics can add huge value to streamlining project management processes and in identifying early warning signs for projects. Being able to parse a discussion thread from your collaboration tool and single out potential risks and issues could change the role of the project manager in the future. Furthermore, natural language searches will make it easier to include narrative discussions, meeting minutes, and more in the data analysis, saving hours of time when investigating or predicting problems. All of this data could be used to predict the future success (or otherwise) of projects.

Allied to the big data revolution is the rise of data presentation techniques, because the trouble with all that data is that it is very difficult to understand. There is a trend toward simple, clean designs for websites and tools with high usability and a very visual impact. The growth of social media sites like Instagram and Pinterest, plus the sudden, recent spike in the number of infographics doing the rounds on sharing sites shows that users are gravitating toward images.

This is relevant to project management collaboration tools because project managers have to adapt the way they communicate to suit the needs of stakeholders. If the needs of stakeholders are evolving to include a requirement for more visuals, then project managers will need to move away from text-based project reports to a more engaging way of sharing status updates.

Visual data presentation is not new to project management—after all, that's really what a Gantt chart is. Kanban, too, is a visual project management approach and many agile teams work with visual plans. We could well see the visual preference for presenting data manifesting itself in more tools that use images and visual workflows in conjunction with traditional Gantt charts.

2. Digital PMOs and the Role of the Digital Leader

Disruptive technologies such as big data are hitting businesses across all functional areas, not just project management. Companies have to come up with practical ways to incorporate this massive amount of change and to sift through the trends that are worth adopting while ditching those that are not relevant at this time. This is starting to come to the fore in the form of the chief digital officer or other digital leadership position at the very top of businesses. We are also seeing digital PMOs—divisions supporting the project structure in the way a traditional PMO would, but with a leaning toward paperless, integrated, and online ways of working, along with the culture changes that brings.

Shadow IT is another challenge for the person or team taking on digital leadership within their organization. This is where employees have downloaded their own apps or software for work purposes. It's common in businesses where IT processes are slow and bureaucratic. When individuals don't want to have to wait for software to be formally approved and installed, the Internet makes it possible for them to download pretty much anything they want and get started immediately. This forces business leaders to look for adaptable, speedy, and flexible models and processes while also giving them the headache of managing data security and unapproved software.

3. The Culture of Collaboration

It's not all about the tech. Part of the challenge facing the digital leader, be that a project manager or a PMO director, will be managing flatter teams, both across business teams and within projects. Employees will create their own internal networks outside of the traditional hierarchy, which potentially makes many of the formal line management structures redundant and forces the organization to become flatter. The digital divide—those employees who are familiar with digital working practices and those who are not—is a further team-related problem that digital leaders have to face up to and proactively manage.

Successful collaboration and teamwork comes from a culture that supports those ways of working. If virtual teams are to be successful, and if collaboration tools are to be fully embedded in the working practices of the team, then it's important for businesses to invest in collaboration offline as well.

We'll see greater investment in building corporate culture, fostering employee engagement, and creating the environment to deliver successful change. All of this underpins the use of any technology and supports the business objective of getting the right people to do the right things the first time, which cuts down on overall project costs.

It also supports the urgent need for knowledge sharing in a global economy that is facing significant talent gaps. As the Baby Boomer generation leaves the workplace, taking with them an incredible amount of organizational knowledge, companies need to find alternative ways to capture and maintain their knowledge assets. Technology (like wikis) has a part to play, as well as collaborative work environments where knowledge is freely shared.

4. Interoperability

You have to invest in keeping your collaboration tools relevant and up-to-date. You should also keep an eye on the future so that if you need to switch systems or link them together, you can. This is interoperability—the ability to use different tools together to provide a single, streamlined technology platform for your company that does not rely on manual rekeying of data.

In my experience, a single platform is better for enterprise data mining, as the fewer interfaces you have to deal with, the easier that exercise is. But it's also unrealistic, especially if your business strategy has been to invest in best-in-class tools for each area instead of a single, "do everything" enterprise product. If you do have multiple systems, interoperability will help you get the data out.

Traditionally, linking systems together has been through data integrators or other pieces of software that built connections and interfaces between various tools, matching up the records and allowing you to transfer data between them. Increasingly in the online space, interoperability is being provided by third-party tools that handle the feeds for you, allowing smaller businesses to get their systems talking to each other without the need for bespoke developments.

Products like Zapier do this. It lets you build "zaps" which effectively work on a "if this happens, do this" basis. For example, if you upload a file to Dropbox, you can automatically sync it to your project management system. More tools are offering application program interfaces (APIs) as well, which are effectively the data standard for that product. By making these standards available, they have done half the integration for you. They let developers build the other half of the integration and match them up, then you can push data into project management tools from other systems and vice versa.

5. Interoperability of Methodology

Businesses don't limit themselves to managing projects using agile or waterfall approaches. The same company can have project managers using PRINCE2®, Scrum, and *A Guide to the Project Management Body of Knowledge (PMBOK® Guide)*. Project collaboration tools need to be flexible enough to deal with all of those methodologies, and to be tailored to support internal processes, as well.

The marketplace today is not full of tools that only support one method, but it is something that decision makers should be aware of— choose a product that supports your future methodology and process needs and not just the approaches you use today.

6. Archiving

One of the other technical challenges of using collaboration tools is how you archive the data effectively. Archiving tools are available, but they are yet another system to integrate within your technology landscape. There's nothing to say that their development will keep up with the constant evolution of the SaaS marketplace; in fact, I think it's fair to say that they aren't.

Forrester reports that only 15% of businesses actively capture and archive data from collaboration sites (Hayes & McKinnon, 2015). The old approaches to data management and records compliance just don't cut it with new communication channels, even where interoperability makes it possible.

This problem is going to get worse before it gets better. Regulatory bodies will catch up with the increase in data being stored across collaboration tools and online and will demand that companies manage their archives more effectively.

Organizations will be forced to adopt more robust methods of managing archives with the associated cost of data management that comes with this. Archiving strategies need to be built in conjunction with the adoption of online tools and with flexibility in mind.

7. Predictive Software

Predictive apps use passive data, for example, emails, to suggest tasks and updates. Think predictive text when you are trying to type a message on your phone, and scale it up so that the app sends suggestions to your to-do list about what activities you should be working on that day or flags which deliverables are likely to be late because of software defects logged in your testing system.

Predictive software sounds like it's taking the thinking and professional judgement out of being a project manager, but it's just crunching data for you. For example, you can't hold information in your head about how accurate each individual team member has been in estimating their workload on this project and the last five projects they have worked on. Predictive software could sift through estimates and actuals, and then flag the three team members with the worst record for getting their estimates right so that you can appropriately challenge them.

This kind of system requires a particular leap of faith as it scours other systems for data. As a community, we're going to have to go a long way before we are all comfortable with the idea of an app reading our emails and digging through personal files, even if it does predict who isn't going to hit their deadlines that week.

Summary

All these trends bode well for both the manufacturers of project management software, and (one would hope) the people using them. Better data, better collaboration, and better end-to-end systems should increase the likelihood of success on projects because it all contributes to better decision making.

Stacy Goff, in the book, *Project Management Circa 2025*, predicts growth in the area of project management software adoption: "A range of innovations (some of which have been on the scene for some time) promises to improve the adoption rate and increase the size of the project management software market," he says. "One such innovation is the combination of virtual teams (project teams that are not colocated) with social networks. Bringing together the tools that support this collaboration and communication reaps great results for those who apply them." (Goff, 2009).

I hope this prediction comes true long before 2025: In fact, collaboration tools are already improving the results of teams where they are being used. However, the great results Goff talks about will only come if the tools being applied meet a genuine business need.

That business need is likely to overlap the areas of technology, collaboration, and culture. The way people work online—both in and outside the project environment—is not perfect, and we can expect to see more evolutions and innovations in the years to come, both in terms of tools and the way in which interactivity is encouraged and fostered.

I hope that we will eventually look back and realize that this decade was the point that organizations made the shift to the collaborative project environment. While the societal change may feel fast, in organizational terms, it is infiltrating slowly. Project leaders are essential in supporting innovation and effective collaboration in all its forms.

Whatever collaboration tools you adopt at work, and however you use them, keep in mind that they should be compatible with and reflect what is going on outside the walls of your company. Technology and workplace cultures will continue to evolve and the key is going to be keeping up and staying relevant while making sure your teams have the tools they need to do their jobs productively.

The future is in flatter, more informal working cultures supported by unified organizational collaborative technologies. We might not refer to the tools that way (or even be using the term social and collaborative media) in ten years' time, but the principles that underpin this revolution in working practices are here to stay.

Appendix

Project Management Resources Online

This is a list of my favorite, current project management social media resources. The web is a fluid place, and blogs, podcasts, and other sites come and go. The blogrolls and links on your favorite bloggers' sites are a good place to start if you are looking for more or new sites.

A Girl's Guide to Project Management

This is my blog, which has been around since 2006. It covers project communication, stakeholder engagement, expert interviews, project management book reviews, and more. I'm the *Girl*, and it's my *Guide* to project management.

http://www.girlsguidetopm.com

Project Management Tips

This is a long-standing, multi-author blog covering a range of project management topics and often touching on online tools.

http://pmtips.net

Better Projects

A blog under the helm of agile expert, Craig Brown. It offers a strong focus on agile and business analysis.

http://www.betterprojects.net

ProjectManagement.com

An active, online community covering a featured topic every month. The discussion groups are particularly good, as are the onsite blogs. I write a blog called "The Money Files" on this site, covering all aspects of project finances. This site is owned and managed by PMI, but you do not have to be a member to join.

http://www.projectmanagement.com

PM Student

This is a blog by Margaret Meloni, which focuses on helping aspiring project managers learn new skills.

http://pmstudent.com

The Practicing IT Project Manager

This blog is written by Dave Gordon, who manages large-scale technology implementations. This includes a weekly roundup of what's new online, which is a great place to start if you are looking for the latest articles and commentators.

http://blog.practicingitpm.com

Project Management Podcast

This is an established podcast hosted by Cornelius Fichtner. There are both free and paid-for versions, which can help you achieve your PDU requirements for your PMI credentials, or just help you learn some interesting stuff. He usually includes an expert interview in most episodes.

http://www.project-management-podcast.com

PM for the Masses

This is a blog and podcast from author Cesar Abeid. It is aimed at demystifying project management topics and sharing lessons from experienced project managers.

http://pmforthemasses.com

Guia de Proyecto

A project management blog in Spanish is written by Danny Reyes.

http://guiadeproyecto.com

EarthPM

This blog is "at the intersection of green and project management" and is run by Cleland-award winning authors, Rich Maltzman and David Shirley.

http://www.earthpm.com

Stepping into Project Management

Still one of my favorite project management blogs, Soma Bhattacharya has been blogging since 2008 and manages to blend project management and lifestyle blogging into an easy-to-read website which also has community elements and free resources.

http://www.steppingintopm.com

Glossary

API: Application Program Interface; a set of rules, protocols, and tools for sending and retrieving data and specifying how elements of software should work together

Archive: Historical log of what has been posted to a blog or other tool; normally organized in date order by month

Big data: The storage and analysis of workplace data for the purpose of creating meaningful management information

Blog: Short for "web log," a type of website in the form of an online diary

Category: Used to catalogue the content on a collaboration tool. For example, a blog about project management may have categories including tips, news, events, risks, schedule information, and so on.

Channel: A mechanism for delivering content. For example, Flickr, the photo sharing site, is a popular channel for sharing and managing photographs

Chat: See instant messaging

Cloud computing: Software tools provided by a third party and hosted online

Comments: Feedback from people who read content on a social media site or collaboration tool. These appear under or are linked to the blog post or other content

Cookie: A small file stored on your computer that stores data like your username and password to avoid having to type it again. Tracking cookies log which websites you have visited and provide marketing data to companies

Emoticon: Symbols created from standard keyboard characters that often look like faces, designed to convey emotion through written text, for example, :)

Emoji: Similar in aim to emoticons, but actually expressed as a picture (e.g., ☺); these are extensions of the character set used by your software

Escrow: A service where an independent third party keeps a copy of the software code on your behalf. You are entitled to use this if your software supplier goes out of business; a risk-mitigation strategy

Feed: A data format for providing information that is frequently updated. It updates automatically so, by always looking in the same place, you can see the latest information

Gamification: Elements of system design and user interface that promote engagement by rewarding certain behaviors and motivating team members to contribute

Host: The server where your collaboration tool is stored; the company you use to serve your collaboration tool

Hyperlink: A piece of text on a web page that directs you to another page when clicked. The standard is for these to appear in blue text and be underlined

Instant messaging: A protocol for a text-based personal conversation online

Interoperability: The ability to use different tools together to provide a single, streamlined technology platform for your company that does not rely on manual rekeying of data

Link: see Hyperlink

Netiquette: Online manners and acceptable behavior for social media interaction. For example, typing in ALL CAPS is perceived as shouting

Page: This is a general term that relates to any content on a website. Typically, it refers to a piece of static content that does not update regularly, as distinct from dynamic "feeds"

PMO: Project management office

Post: Usually an entry in a blog, but can be used as a generic term for content on other types of collaboration tool. Also "to post:" the act of uploading information to an online system

Podcast: An audio recording; an online radio show that can be downloaded and listened to on the move through an MP3 player or via the computer

Presence: The ability to know if someone is available to be contacted in real time

RSS: Really simple syndication

Smileys: See Emoticon

Software as a Service (SaaS): Software provided by a third party as a complete solution, including hosting and maintenance. The purchaser pays a licence fee for use of the software, but everything else is managed by the third party

Tag: A way of categorizing content. Tags can be any words describing the content and are used by search engines to find and sort relevant information

Two-factor authentication: Method of logging into a software tool that involves a username, password, and a code that is randomly generated at the moment you log in and then expires shortly afterward. This could be sent by text or generated via an app.

URL: Uniform resource locator; the syntax that describes where to find something online

Wiki: A collection of web pages acting as a hyperlinked knowledge repository and data set

References

AMA/ePolicy Institute. (2009). *Electronic business communication policies & procedures survey*. Retrieved 30 June 2015 from http://www .epolicyinstitute.com/2009-electronic-business-communication-policies-procedures-survey-results

Barefoot, D. & Szabo, J. (2010). *Friends with benefits: A social media marketing handbook*. (pp. 7-8). San Francisco, CA: No Starch Press.

Bernoff, J., Riley, E., Pflaum, C., Cummings, T., Polanco, A., & Wise, J. (2010, January 15). *Introducing the new social technographics®: How conversationalists change the marketing landscape*. Forrester Research. Retrieved 11 February 2016 from https://www.forrester.com/Introducing+The+New+Social+Technographics/fulltext/-/E-res56291#AST114299

Besner, C., & Hobbs, B. (2013). Contextualization of project management practice: A cluster analysis of practices and best practices. *Project Management Journal, 44*(1), 17–34.

Bloch, S., & Whiteley, P. (2009). *How to manage in a flat world: 10 strategies to get connected to your team wherever they are*. Upper Saddle River, NJ: FT Press.

Bughin, J. & Chui, M. (2010, December). The rise of the networked enterprise: Web 2.0 finds its payday. *McKinsey Quarterly*. Retrieved 21 July 2015 from http://www.mckinsey.com/insights/high_tech_telecoms_internet/the_rise_of_the_networked_enterprise_web_20_finds_its_payday

CareerBuilder.com. (2015, July 2). *Employers reveal the top factors preventing workers' chance of promotion in new CareerBuilder survey*. Retrieved from http://www.careerbuilder.co.uk/share/aboutus/pressreleasesdetail.aspx?sd=7%2f2%2f2015&siteid=cbpr&sc_cmp1=cb_pr901_&id=pr901&ed=12%2f31%2f2015

CERFDOE Final Report – 071204. (2004). Independent research assessment of project management factors affecting Department of Energy project success. *Civil Engineering Research Foundation*, United States, p. 18.

Chiu, M., Manyika, J., Bughin, J., Dobbs, R., Roxburgh, C., Sarrazin, H., Sands, G., & Westergren, M. (2012, July). The social economy: Unlocking value and productivity through social technologies. *McKinsey Global Institute*. Retrieved 1 March 2015

Cloud Security Alliance. (2015, January). *Cloud adoption practices and priorities survey report*. Retrieved 31 August 2015 from http://bitly/1IgnqK9

Crusan, J. (2015, May-June). Light-touch management with social media. *Research-Technology Management Journal, 58*(3), 68.

Deloitte. (2013). *Digital collaboration: Delivering innovation, productivity and happiness*. Retrieved 31 August 2015 from http://www2.deloitte .com/content/dam/Deloitte/se/Documents/technology-media-telecommunications/deloitte-digital-collaboration.pdf

Dolan, C. (2013). *Investigation of the uses of social media in a project environment, and the quantification of the benefits of applying social media paradigms to a project environment*. Unpublished Master's Thesis. Retrieved 31 August 2015 from http://figshare.com/articles/ Social_Media_uses_in_Project_Management_pdf/1447155

Goff, S. (2009). Visions for the project management software industry. In D. I. Cleland & B. Bidanda (Eds.), *Project management circa 2025,* (p. 173). Newtown Square, PA: Project Management Institute.

Hayes, N., & McKinnon, C. (2015, March 9). Market overview: Social media archiving. *Forrester Research, Inc.* Retrieved 31 August 2015 from http:// www2.smarsh.com/2015-Forrester-Market-Overview-Social-Media

Howard, C., Natis, Y. V., Harris-Ferrante, K., Proctor, P. E., Cain, M. W., Rollings, M., Thomas, A., Gotta, M., & Anderson, E. (2014, February 28). *Transform your business with the Nexus of Forces*. Gartner. Retrieved 27 February 2015 from https://www.gartner .com/doc/2673815 28

Ipsos. (2013, January 8). Socialogue: The most common butterfly on earth is the social butterfly. *Ipsos.* Retrieved 31 August 2015 from http://ipsos-na.com/news-polls/pressrelease.aspx?id=5954

Jaafari, A. (2003, December). Project management in the age of complexity and change. *Project Management Journal, 34*(4), 47–57.

Kiron, D., Palmer, D., Nguyen Phillips, A., & Berkman, R. (2013, July 16). Social business: Shifting out of first gear. *MIT Sloan Management Review* and *Deloitte University Press.* Retrieved 1 March 2015 from http://cdn.dupress.com/wp-content/uploads/2013/07/DUP446_SB_Report_Final.pdf

Leadbeater, C. (2009). We-Think: Mass innovation, not mass production. London, UK: Profile Books.

Major Projects Association. (2015, June 17). *Developing a digital strategy for major projects.* Highlights from the Major Projects Association event. Retrieved 31 August 2015 from http://www.majorprojects.org/pdf/highlights/193highlightsdigitalstrategy.pdf

Moore, S. (2010). *Strategic project portfolio management.* Hoboken, NJ: Wiley.

Murch, R. (2001). *Project management: Best practices for IT professionals.* Upper Saddle River, NJ: Prentice Hall.

Paroutis, S., & Al Saleh, A. (2009). Determinants of knowledge sharing using Web 2.0 technologies. *Journal of Knowledge Management, 13*(4), 52–63.

Phillips, D. (2008, October). The psychology of social media. *Journal of New Communications Research, 3*(1), 81–82.

Project Management Institute. (2013, March). *PMI talent gap report.* Newtown Square, PA: Author. Retrieved 24 July 2015 from http://www.pmi.org/~/media/PDF/Business-Solutions/PMIProjectManagementSkillsGapReport.ashx

Projectplace. (n. d.). *The chaos theory.* Retrieved 24 July 2015 from https://www.projectplace.com/Global/pdf/whitepaper/EN/Ebook-chaos-theory-en.pdf

Proskauer. (n. d.). Social media in the workplace around the world 3.0. *2013/14 survey.* Retrieved 30 June 2015 from http://www.proskauer.com/files/uploads/social-media-in-the-workplace-2014.pdf

Purcell, K., & Rainie, L. (2014, December 30). Technology's impact on workers. *Pew Research Center.* Retrieved 31 August 2015 from http://www.pewinternet.org/2014/12/30/technologys-impact-on-workers/

Scott, L. (2013, September 26). LinkedIn for project management. *Arras People Benchmark Report.* Retrieved 3 August 2015 from http://www.arraspeople.co.uk/camel-blog/projectmanagement/linkedin-for-project-management/

Simon, P. (2015). *Message not received.* Hoboken, NJ: Wiley.

Stang, D. B., Handler, R. A., & Jones, T. (2015, May 20). Magic quadrant for IT project and portfolio management software applications, world-wide. *Gartner.* Retrieved 31 August 2015 from http://bit.ly/1LNMQA9

Tapscott, D., & Williams, A. D. (2008). *Wikinomics: How mass collaboration changes everything.* London, UK: Atlantic Books.

Thamhain, H. (2009). The future of team leadership in complex project environments. In *Project management circa 2025*, D. I. Cleland & B. Bidanda. (Eds.), (pp. 368–369). Newtown Square, PA: Project Management Institute.

Wagner, T. (2015, January 27). Doing the numbers on the northeast's snowstorm. *Planalytics.* Retrieved 8 February 2016 from http://bit.ly/1O47RE4

Wearne, S. & White-Hunt, K. (2014). *Managing the urgent and unexpected.* Farnham, UK: Gower.

Westerman, G., Bonnet, D., & McAfee, A. (2014). *Leading digital: Turning technology into business transformation*. Boston, MA: Harvard Business Review Press.

Westerman, G., Tannou, M., Bonnet, D., Ferraris,P., & McAfee, A. (n. d.). The digital advantage: How digital leaders outperform their peers in every industry. *Capgemini Consulting*. Retrieved 24 July 2015 from https://www.capgemini.com/resource-file-access/resource/pdf/ The_Digital_Advantage_How_Digital_Leaders_Outperform_their_ Peers_in_Every_Industry.pdf

Wible, A. (2009). Use a wiki. In B. Davis (Ed.), *97 things every project manager should know*. (pp. 50–51). Sebastopol, CA: O'Reilly Media.

Wise, T. P. (2013). *Trust in virtual teams*. Farnham, UK: Gower.

Suggested Reading

Throughout the book I have referenced articles, studies, and books that I have found particularly relevant. Here is a final selection of further reading that I recommend to continue your investigations into virtual and digital ways of working.

Working with Technology

Flynn, N. (2009). *The e-policy handbook.* (2nd ed.). New York, NY: AMACOM.

Sampson, G. (2008). *Electronic business.* Swindon, UK: BCS.

Communication

Bourne, L. (2012). *Advising upwards: A framework for understanding and engaging senior management stakeholders.* Farnham, UK: Gower.

Erwin, K. (2014). *Communicating the new: Methods to shape and accelerate innovation.* Hoboken, NJ: Wiley.

Franklin, M., & Tuttle, S. (2008). *Communication skills for project and programme managers.* London, UK: TSO.

Mersino, A. (2013). *Emotional intelligence for project managers: The people skills you need to achieve outstanding results.* (2nd ed.). New York, NY: AMACOM.

Team Management

Bloch, S., & Whitely, P. (2009). *How to manage in a flat world: 10 strategies to get connected to your team wherever they are.* Upper Saddle River, NJ: FT Press.

Franklin, M., & Tuttle, S. (2008). *Team management skills for project and programme managers.* London, UK: TSO.

Garton C., & Wegryn, K. (2006). *Managing without walls: Maximize success with virtual, global, and cross-cultural teams.* Lewisville, TX: M C Press.

Pullan, P. (2016). Virtual leadership: Practical strategies for getting the best out of virtual work and virtual teams. London, UK: Kogan Page.

Tuckman, B. W. (1965). Development sequence in small groups. *Psychological Bulletin 63,* 284–299.

Wise, T. P. (2013). *Trust in virtual teams.* Farnham, UK: Gower.

Social Media and Collaboration

Barefoot, D. & Szabo, J. (2010). *Friends with benefits: A social media marketing handbook.* San Francisco, CA: No Starch Press.

Coiné, T. & Babbitt, M. (2014). *A world gone social: How companies must adapt to survive.* New York, NY: AMACOM.

Howe, J. (2008). *Crowdsourcing: How the power of the crowd is driving the future of business.* London, UK: Random House.

Leadbeater, C. (2009). *We-think: Mass innovation, not mass production.* London, UK: Profile Books.

Surowiecki, J. (2004). *The wisdom of crowds.* London, UK: Little, Brown.

Tabaka, J. (2006). *Collaboration explained: Facilitation skills for software project leaders.* Upper Saddle River, NJ: Addison Wesley.

Tapscott, D., & Williams, A. D. (2008). *Wikinomics: How mass collaboration changes everything, expanded edition.* London, UK: Atlantic.

Zarrella, D. (2010). *The social media marketing book.* Sebastopol, CA: O'Reilly.

Project Management

Berkun, S. (2008). *Making things happen: Mastering project management.* Sebastopol, CA: O'Reilly.

Cleland, D. I., & Bidanda, B. (Eds.). (2009). *Project management circa 2025.* Newtown Square, PA: Project Management Institute.

Furman, J. (2015). *The project management answer book.* (2nd ed.). Vienna, Austria: Management Concepts.

Harrin, E. (2013). *Shortcuts to success: Project management in the real world.* (2nd ed.). Swindon, UK: BCS.

Kerzner, H. R. (2015), *Project management 2.0.* Hoboken, NJ: Wiley.

Moore, S. (2010). *Strategic project portfolio management.* Hoboken, NJ: Wiley.

Project Management Institute. (2013). *A guide to the project management body of knowledge (PMBOK guide®) – Fifth edition.* Newtown Square, PA: Author.

About the Author

ELIZABETH HARRIN, MA, FAPM, MBCS is director of Otobos Consultants Ltd., a project communications consultancy specializing in copywriting for project management firms. Ms. Harrin also works as a practicing project and program manager. She spent eight years working in financial services (including two based in Paris, France) before moving into healthcare.

She is a PRINCE2, MSP, and P3O Practitioner, and holds the ITIL Foundation certificate. She is a Fellow of the Association for Project Management and a member of the Project Management Institute (PMI). She holds degrees from The University of York and Roehampton University.

She is the author of three books about project management: *Shortcuts to Success: Project Management in the Real World* (which was a finalist in the Management Book of the Year Awards 2014), *Social Media for Project Managers,* and *Customer-Centric Project Management.* She has also produced several ebooks and an online course on project reporting.

She's particularly interested in stakeholder engagement and team communications and offers coaching to mid-level project managers looking to improve their skills.

Ms. Harrin is the award-winning blogger behind A Girl's Guide to Project Management, a specialist blog aimed at helping project managers communicate more effectively. She is widely published on project management topics and has contributed to numerous websites and magazines.

Website: www.GirlsGuidetoPM.com
Twitter: @pm4girls.

Other Books by Elizabeth Harrin

Customer-Centric Project Management
Shortcuts to Success: Project Management in the Real World
Social Media for Project Managers
Customer-Centric Project Management, with Phil Peplow

Some short sections of this book originally appeared online.

Praise for Collaboration Tools for Project Managers

"The book provides an excellent overview for managers at all levels in an organization of how collaboration tools can be utilized in project environments. This is a very hot topic. Talking to different companies about the challenges they face in managing their projects effectively and efficiently, it is clear to me that a key piece of the jigsaw is the utilization of the types of collaboration tools that Elizabeth refers to."

Professor David Bryde, Liverpool Business School,
Liverpool John Moores University

"The right project management software can make a huge difference to the success of project teams by helping the team collaborate and thrive. Yet we know companies find it hard to break away from their historical tool sets and embrace online and collaborative tools. This book makes it easy. It's a step by step guide to choosing a product that's going to work for you and your team, with advice on setting it up, increasing adoption and making decisions that support collaborative working across teams. Whether you're deciding on an online tool for the first time or want to move to a new one, this book will ensure that you boost productivity and get the most from any new social tools."

Liz Pearce, CEO LiquidPlanner

"As project managers, we can no longer just manage our project details: schedule, budget, quality, scope. Yes, they do need to be managed, but it is becoming much more than that. One must, as Elizabeth says 'create collaborative environments where people can do their best work. . . .' That environment will not only make the project manager more effective, but will make the project more successful, something we all strive for. In her book, *Collaboration Tools for Project Management*, Elizabeth does just that—help the project manager use all the collaborative tools available. She defines the tools, provides the reasoning behind their effectiveness, and explains how to use them for their maximum value. Elizabeth also provides a road map to a myriad of resources as well as inviting the reader into the conversation. This book is a must read for all project managers who want to be more effective, and I believe that is what we all want."

David Shirley, PMP, author, educator, and
2011 Cleland Project Management
Literature Award Winner